MARIO BATALI
ITALIAN GRILL

MARIO BATALI
ITALIAN GRILL

with Judith Sutton

PHOTOGRAPHY BY
Beatriz da Costa

ART DIRECTION BY
Lisa Eaton and Douglas Riccardi

ecco

An Imprint of HarperCollinsPublishers

ALSO BY MARIO BATALI

Molto Italiano

Mario Tailgates NASCAR Style

The Babbo Cookbook

Holiday Food

Simple Italian Food

Designed by Memo Productions, NY

All photography © 2008 by Beatriz da Costa, except for the photographs on the following pages, which are © 2008 by Joe Vaughn: v, vi, viii, 10, 13, 41, 51, 65, 91, 104, 109, 139, 155, 162, 189, 202, 228.

ISBN: 978-0-06-145097-6

THIS BOOK IS DEDICATED TO

LEO, BENNO, AND SUSI,

THE HOTTEST COALS ON MY GRILL

ACKNOWLEDGMENTS

I would like to give special thanks to the following people who made this book possible:

First of all, **SUSI, BENNO, AND LEO,** for putting up with all of the food and folks in the house during the photo shoot

My partner, **JOE BASTIANICH,** for continuing to push and pull us forward in the real business

THE MANAGEMENT TEAMS at Babbo, Lupa, Esca, Otto, Casa Mono, Bar Jamón, The Spotted Pig, Del Posto, Pizzeria and Osteria Mozza, B & B Ristorante, Enoteca San Marco, and Carnevino, where the real deal happens every day all day and we love it

PAM LEWY, for taking on the foolishness of FedEx and other lions with a smile and a shotgun

LISA EATON, for purity and truth

DOUGLAS RICCARDI, for the design

KRISTA AND REX RUANE, for the food styling

CAMMIE BUEHLER AND ANDY SCHUDLICH, for truly bringing on the noise in the kitchen

BEA DA COSTA AND MEGAN SENIOR, for truth and light on the page

SUSIE THEODOREAU, for the beautiful plates and other props

JUDITH SUTTON, for all her hard work on the book, including recipe testing

DANIEL HALPERN AND EMILY TAKOUDES at Ecco, for keeping it real in the publishing world

My agent, **TONY GARDNER,** and my lawyer, **CATHY FRANKEL,** for truth and consistency

FRIEDA'S SPECIALTY PRODUCE, for delicious vegetables for the photos

VIKING AND KITCHENAID, for always being there when I ask

JUAN MIGUEL, AND TOOTS, for the comedy

MY PARTNERS at Copco, Crocs, Ernst Benz, and General Mills, for being cool about everything

And **JIM HARRISON,** for the fun with a gun and rod, the real first step to a good grill

Judith Sutton would like to thank:

My sister, **ANN,** for major kitchen prep

SHARON AND DAVID BOWERS, for help with recipe testing

All my recipe taste-testers, including friends and family

And **MARIO BATALI,** who is always great to work with, even when he's opening a couple of new restaurants and is involved in a hundred other projects

INTRODUCTION

The words "Italian" and "grilling" go together like the verse and refrain in a love song by Lennon and McCartney—they seem as if they were made for each other. Anyone who has spent any time at all in the real Italy knows that many of the most evocative and fragrant moments are sniffed at someone's house, or in a vineyard, or at a trattoria where something delicious is cooking on a grill over hot coals. The kiss of the fire and iron grate can transform even the most quotidian vegetables or meats or fish into that hauntingly elusive perfect bite where the flavor of the natural product is enhanced, not masked, and the garden or the sea or the butcher shop and the flame unite to create an aria of flavor that renders worthy any effort it takes to get to the very point of enjoying it.

Yet America is a wild world of grill experts. We practically invented the backyard cookout, and we certainly invented the complex national fabric of real barbecue in its infinite permutations across our back roads and small towns from the Carolinas to California, from Texas to Toronto. Everything from weenie roasts to clambakes forms the vernacular of the American grill and the regional variations that make it our specialty. We all know how to grill—we were born with it; it is ours.

Still, Italian grilling is not so different from ours in its intention. The Italian grill is all about nuance and minimal interference with the flavor of the primary ingredient. There is no thick sweet barbecue sauce, no sweet-and-sour glaze, nothing kicked up a notch or two, and minimal basting (if any) in the Italian kitchen. Marinades are important, but they are lighter and certainly have no soy or teriyaki, or Tabasco and buttermilk baths. There is rarely anything more to them than good olive oil, citrus, wine, herbs, garlic, and hot chili flakes.

The recipes I offer in the following pages are not exactly 100 percent Italian. I celebrate the idea of the American mastery of the backyard grill, and I do love a kick-ass barbecue sauce. I will use a slightly sweet glaze on porchetta, that Italian icon, and there is a little zip in the dry rub for my rib eye. But the true Italian ideology is neither obfuscated nor watered down. What you will find here is my take on the Italian grill, just as I have always passed the world of Italian cooking through my rose-colored glasses, through my own culinary prism.

ITALIAN WINES FOR GRILLING

BY DAVID LYNCH

Choosing wines for grilled foods offers the wine guy a rare opportunity to be macho. Most of the time we are sniffing for subtleties, cooing over complexity, babbling about balance. The barbecue is a time to be bold—to fight fire with fire, or, as the Italians would put it, *fuoco al fuoco*.

Even when he isn't grilling, of course, Mario brings the heat. When I was the sommelier at Babbo, I once had the temerity to request less chili flake in a pasta dish to make it more wine-friendly (hot spices amplify the heat of alcohol and tannin). I don't remember his response exactly, but I think he threw a pinch more *peperoncini* into the pan, planted a defiant fist on his hip, and let loose a menacing cackle, like a pirate.

The lesson? Be bold, or stay out of the way. This is how I've come to approach most wine-and-food pairings, but it is an especially good mantra when firing up the grill. Whether it's a blast of lemon juice on a swordfish steak or some serious fat marbling in a rib eye—not to mention the smoky, sharp taste of char, which is to be your constant companion as you work through this book—the typical grill preparation has strong flavors and textures, and the wine should offer the same in return.

Let's start with *vini bianchi*. Grilling presents an opportunity to break out some fatter, barrel-fermented Italian whites—a "super-white" Friulian blend, perhaps, or maybe a big-name Chardonnay from Tuscany or Piedmont. You may have been saving such wines to show off at a fussier, more "special" occasion, but they might actually show their best around the grill. Think of how well a big Chardonnay-based white such as Antinori's Cervaro della Sala or Joe Bastianich's Vespa Bianco would complement the toasty, bready flavors of grilled polenta or pizza. You'll also crave some vinous viscosity with richer seafoods like lobster, salmon, and especially monkfish. These days it's fashionable to dismiss oaky wines as being overpowering, but add some grill char and other big flavors to the equation, and suddenly a little wood toast and weight is just what you need.

More than anything else, however, what you'll need from whites is acidity. There's a lot of citrus in these recipes—Fennel with Sambuca and Grapefruit, Baby Octopus with Olive-Orange Vinaigrette, Lobster with Lemon Oil—so while it's nice to have a wine with big flavor, it can't be flabby. It needs to have grip, if for no other reason than to battle all that lemon or other citrus juice, and, of course, there's a difference between a white wine that is simply acidic and one that has actual flavor and structure. When I'm looking for bold flavor combined with a good backbone of acidity, I look to Vermentino di Sardegna (lots of pungent green-herb notes for all the mint and thyme you'll find in these recipes); Pinot Bianco from the Alto Adige (a nice, rich, almost Chardonnay-like feel, but usually without the oak); Tocai Friulano from Friuli (great minerality and Sauvignon-like grassiness, perfect for the likes of Calamari Spiedini in Lemon Leaves and the Warm Shrimp Salad, among others); and Fiano di Avellino from Campania (also a little minty and herbal, with a jolt of citrus).

On the red side, my go-to barbecue wine is Montepulciano d'Abruzzo. It's big and bold, with a satisfyingly deep color and tons of rich fruit, yet the tannins are nice and soft, so as not to fight with the char—or the black pepper, or the chili pepper flakes, or whatever heat-inducing item Mario chooses to throw at you. Although there are many instances where I'd go with some blunt-force tannins—what else but a burly, tannic Brunello di Montalcino with *bistecca alla fiorentina*—there are plenty of big, meaty Italian reds with softer contours. If you haven't yet turned on to the tarry Teroldegos of Trentino, or to the exceedingly funky Lagreins of Alto Adige, there is no better time to do so than when you're grilling meat; these wines actually taste a little charred around the edges (I'm not kidding).

Other good all-purpose grilling reds would include Carignano del Sulcis, from Sardegna (I'd pair this rustic red with the Spit-Roasted Leg of Lamb and sit down in the grass and eat like a Sardinian shepherd);

Barbera d'Alba, from Piedmont (a little more acidic tang and brightness and thus workable with lots of the poultry preparations); and any number of bold, fruity *rosatos* from all over the boot, which are great for taming peppery heat but counterpunching with flavor. (Mario's wife, Susi, is partial to the fey, copper-colored rosés of Bandol in France, and she has hated every single gutsy Italian rosé I've served her over the years, but I remain undaunted in my support for Italian *rosato*, especially in this char-broiled context!)

Is there ever an instance where you wouldn't be bold? Well, if you've got a lot of chili heat in a preparation or a generous coating of black pepper, your best wine may be the less assertive one: go with something crisp, soft, cooling, something that's content to clean up after the dish rather than engage it in a debate. With whites, opt for no oak, bright acidity, low alcohol—and there's plenty of squeaky-clean, high-acid Italian juice out there when you decide to "stay out of the way." With reds, choose lower alcohol, softer tannins, refreshing fruit. Some of the more easygoing choices would include non-riserva Chianti Classico from Tuscany, a Cerasuolo di Vittoria from Sicily, and maybe a Valpolicella from the Veneto.

In the end, your best bet is to think big and throw caution to the winds. Maybe toss the Brunello on ice to tone down its tannins, then let 'er rip! It's a barbecue—don't be such a wine geek.

GRILLING BASICS

Grilling over hot coals or embers is as timeless as cooking itself, in Italy and the world throughout. For the purest, most unadorned, and primordial experience, it's the grill. The uniquely satisfying seasoning and delicious flavor that the smoldering fire and its smoke create is quite simply unattainable with any other method of heat transfer. This chapter covers what I consider the few but crucial basics for making well-informed decisions about your own grilling style.

CHOOSING A GRILL

The big decision, of course, is gas versus charcoal. The obvious advantage of a gas grill is convenience, and gas grills now outsell charcoal grills in the United States. The fire will be ready in 10 to 15 minutes, as opposed to the 25 or 30 charcoal takes, and it will burn for as long as you leave the grill on. Cleanup is easy, and a gas grill is also more economical in the long run. And because it's so easy, if you have a gas grill, you may find yourself grilling throughout much more of the year, even when it starts to turn cold.

Gas grills are fueled by either a natural-gas hookup or a small propane tank. If you use propane, be sure to have a backup tank ready and waiting (store it in a cool, shaded place outside, away from the grill). Older gas grills had only two side-by-side burners. Now many models have three burners, and their configuration varies widely. If you often grill for a crowd, you may want a big three-burner grill,

but a good-sized two-burner version is more than adequate for most purposes. While it's true that gas grills tend to burn less hot than a charcoal fire, they are becoming more powerful. And instead of the ceramic briquettes or lava rocks used in older grills, many newer models include features designed to add to the grilled flavor, such as metal slats positioned between the burners and the grate to catch the juices from the grilling food—as the juices drip onto the hot metal and caramelize or evaporate, their smoky perfume fills the grill.

Many hard-core grill dogs and barbecuers disdain gas grills, insisting that food cooked over a gas flame doesn't have the same flavor as that cooked over live fire and that turning on a gas grill just isn't "real" grilling. It's true that building a live fire is a more hands-on experience, and that a steak cooked over a real hardwood fire will have more char flavor than one cooked on a gas grill. But in reality, most people use charcoal briquettes, and even if you use hardwood lump charcoal, the difference in flavor is likely to be minimal. The main disadvantage of a charcoal grill is the limited window of grilling time. For foods that take longer than about 20 to 30 minutes to cook, you can add more coals to the fire (20 or so at a time) as it burns, but you have to keep your eye on the fire and the time.

Kettle grills are the most popular type of charcoal grill. They have two racks, the grill grate and another one for the coals. A disadvantage of most kettle grills is that the grill rack has only one position, so you can't lower or raise it to change the heat level. Square or rectangular charcoal grills may not have a separate grate for the coals, but they usually have at least two positions for the grill rack.

Portable grills can be handy for picnics or tailgating. Both gas and charcoal versions are available. Portable charcoal grills include tabletop models and the familiar hibachi.

If you grill a lot and have the space, you might want to have both a gas grill and a charcoal one. Or, for the real experience, get either a gas or a charcoal grill and then build a wood-burning brick oven in the backyard—like the one I have at my summer house.

LIGHTING THE FIRE

If you have a gas grill, all you need to do is turn it on or ignite the flame. Always have the lid of the grill open when you turn on the fuel, or gas could build up and cause an explosion; also check to make sure that all the burners have ignited before you close the lid to allow the grill to preheat. Let the grill preheat, with all the burners on high, for 10 to 15 minutes, then adjust the burner heat if necessary, depending on what you are cooking.

The easiest way to light a fire in a charcoal grill is to use a chimney, a simple metal cylinder with a wire grate toward the bottom and four vent holes. Crumple a few pieces of newspaper and stuff them into the bottom of the chimney, set it on the bottom grill grate or the bottom of the grill, and fill it with charcoal. Open all the vents in the bottom of the grill, light the newspaper through the vent holes in the chimney, and watch to make sure it has ignited the charcoal—you should see flames reaching up through the briquettes (if not, replace the newspaper and light it again). Wait until all the coals are ignited, usually

about 15 minutes, then carefully pour them out into the grill and let burn until they are all covered with grayish-white ash.

Electric coil starters, available at hardware stores, are another option for lighting a charcoal fire. Place the starter on the bottom grill grate or the bottom of the grill, carefully pile the charcoal on top of it, and plug it in. Once the coals have ignited, after about 10 minutes, carefully remove the starter and set it on a heatproof surface (somewhere safe, where no one might touch it) to cool down. You can add more coals to the ones that have ignited if you want a larger fire. Then let them all burn until covered with ash.

You can also use paraffin starters, available at most hardware stores, to ignite the charcoal (these can replace the newspaper in a chimney starter). Simply follow the instructions on the package. But avoid lighter fluid at all costs. It smells terrible and it can add its unmistakable flavor to the food. Avoid self-igniting briquettes for the same reason.

Regular charcoal briquettes are made of pulverized and compressed hardwood charcoal and chemical binders. The more expensive brands tend to burn longer than the generics. Hardwood charcoal, called natural lump charcoal or charwood, is made from various hardwoods, including hickory, mesquite, and oak, and contains no additives. It burns faster and hotter than charcoal briquettes, and it is more expensive, so use it for cooking steaks and other meats where you want a good sear and the cooking time is relatively short.

WOOD CHIPS AND CHUNKS

Wood chips or chunks are an easy way to add a smoky flavor to grilled meats such as pork tenderloin and steaks. Mesquite, hickory, and oak chips are the most widely available, but other hardwoods are used as well. Soak wood chips in water for at least 30 minutes before using, chunks for at least an hour. If using a charcoal grill, just scatter the wood over the hot coals. Some gas grills come equipped with a smoker drawer or a metal chip holder. If yours doesn't have one, wrap the chips or chunks in heavy-duty foil and poke some holes in it; set the packet directly on one of the burners. You can also flavor meats with strong herbs such as rosemary (see Ribs Italian-Style, page 190). Stalks of dried wild fennel are often thrown onto the fire in Italy and other parts of the Mediterranean, as are grapevine cuttings.

GRILLING TECHNIQUES

Cover the grill! You may be tempted to keep a close eye on that big juicy steak as it cooks, but, in a word, don't. With the exception of thin fish fillets, sliced vegetables, and other foods that cook very quickly, almost everything should be cooked with the grill lid down, to keep the heat and flavorful smoke inside. You could think of covered grilling as roasting over coals. And remember that there's no need to keep turning and moving the food around as it cooks, except to avoid flare-ups (you'll notice in fact that many of my recipes say to "cook, unmoved, until . . . "). When searing meat, give it a chance to develop nice dark grill marks. No matter what you are grilling, it will cook more evenly and more quickly if you leave it alone—turn it only once, or as directed in the recipe.

Some of the recipes in this book tell you to oil the grill before putting the food on it. You can use a long-handled basting brush or a clean rag dipped in oil to do this (you may want to hold the rag with tongs). Lightly oil the grate just before putting the food on it. In some cases, you may need to brush the food with oil too—or oil the food instead of the grate.

DIRECT AND INDIRECT GRILLING

Although a hot fire is essential for many recipes, not everything should be grilled over high heat. And some foods, such as big cuts of meat and whole birds, should be grilled over indirect heat so they can cook to the desired doneness without incinerating the outside. Some recipes use both direct and indirect heat: a piece of meat may be seared over the hottest part of the grill, for example, then moved to the cooler part to cook through.

Grilling over direct heat means cooking the food over the hottest part of the fire. It's what you want for thinner cuts, for fish and shellfish, cut-up chicken, sliced vegetables—i.e., food that cooks quickly. Cook over direct heat when you want to sear the food, giving it great color and a delicious flavor. For direct cooking on a gas grill, after preheating the grill, leave all the burners on high, put the food on the grill, and cook as directed. For a charcoal grill, leave the coals in a mound for very intense heat, or spread them out a bit if you need a larger cooking area. Have all the vents open so there is plenty of oxygen to feed the flames.

For indirect cooking on a gas grill, preheat all the burners on high, then turn off the center burner if you have three, or one of the burners if you have two. If the recipe calls for it, turn the other burner(s) down. Put the food over the cooler part of the grill to cook—and be sure to cover the grill. There are various options for cooking over indirect heat in a charcoal grill. The simplest is to move all the hot coals to one side of the grill and cook the food on the other, cooler side. Or divide the coals and mound them on two opposite sides of the grill, leaving the center bare, and cook over the center part. In either case, it's a good idea to put a drip pan filled with a little water under the cooler part of the grill to prevent the drippings from burning. A third option, if you are cooking something like chicken thighs (such as Chicken Thighs with Snap Peas and *Agliata*, page 141), is to leave the hot coals in the center of the grill and arrange the food around the cooler perimeter.

CROSSHATCHING

If you've ever wondered how chefs make those beautiful patterns of grill marks that adorn grilled salmon fillets and fish steaks, chicken breasts, and other cuts, it's actually really easy. Put the food on the grill and let it sear or cook long enough to get well-charred grill marks. Rotate it 90 degrees and cook a few minutes longer, and you will have that distinctive crosshatch pattern. Turn the food over and continue cooking as directed.

SPIT-ROASTING

If you have never tried spit-roasting because you think it is difficult, expensive, and/or intimidating, you will be surprised to find that it's none of these: it's really easy, a rotisserie attachment is by no means a huge investment, and spit-roasting is lots of fun! The results are delicious, and the technique—and delicious results—will amaze and impress your guests. Some high-end gas grills come with a rotisserie attachment, and many manufacturers offer an attachment as an option. Relatively inexpensive models that fit most grills (charcoal as well as gas) can be purchased online or at some hardware stores. In any case, you'll want to buy a well-constructed model with a sturdy spit that can support big birds and roasts. Fortunately we no longer have to turn

the spit by hand—nowadays a small electric motor, attached to one side of the grill, does all the work. You simply skewer the food on the spit, securing it with the clamps that are part of the setup, lay the spit over the grill, and insert the end of it into the motor housing. Cover the grill and turn on the motor—that's all there is to it!

You'll need to review the specific instructions for the model you buy (and check your grill manual for additional information), but basically spit-roasted food is cooked over indirect heat in a covered grill. Generally the food should be brought to room temperature before it is grilled, since it will not be cooking at a high temperature. Be sure to set up a drip pan under the center of the rotisserie to catch the juices; you may need to pour a little water or other liquid, such as wine, into the pan to prevent the drippings from burning.

COOKING ON A PIASTRA

Cooking on a piastra is a time-honored technique throughout Italy, especially in Friuli and along the Adriatic Coast. *Alla piastra* essentially means cooking on a flat griddle over a hot fire, and the same method is popular throughout the Mediterranean. Cooking *a la plancha* is a favorite way of preparing fish in Spain, and in Greece, cooking on a *satz*, a sheet of metal, is centuries old. Today the free-form sheets of metal used in ancient times have mostly been replaced by griddles made of cast iron or another metal. You could use a regular stovetop griddle with a smooth surface as a piastra. These are readily available in housewares shops, some hardware stores, and online; a large rectangular griddle that fits over two burners is a good choice. An old-fashioned cast-iron pancake griddle would also work, although these are on the smaller

side, or even a quarter-inch-thick slab of slate. But best of all is my piastra (see www.italian kitchen.com), which is made of thin but durable, and remarkably light, granite and, at 10 inches by 14 inches, gives you a generous cooking area.

The advantage of a piastra is that it gives you a very hot cooking surface—hot enough to make mussels dance when they are tossed onto it (see Mussels alla Piastra with Prosciutto Bread Crumbs, page 96). It's a fun and easy way to cook many foods from shrimp (see page 101) to calamari (see page 93). I also use one to "grill-bake" flatbreads such as schiacciate (pages 76 and 79). Just be sure to give the piastra enough time to get really hot—let it preheat, covered, on the hot grill for at least 10 to 15 minutes.

FIRE-ROASTING

Fire-roasting refers to cooking in the hot coals of a wood or charcoal fire. It's a popular method in Italy, used to cook vegetables while a large cut of meat—or even a whole pig or lamb—cooks slowly over a fire. Whole potatoes, onions, beets, or other vegetables are placed in the coals around the perimeter of the fire to roast in their skins. Big globe artichokes are a natural for this, as the inedible outer leaves char and burn away in the heat of the fire, leaving the tender inner leaves and heart, which will have essentially steamed in their own juices. To cook more delicate vegetables, such as corn, fennel, or new potatoes, wrap them individually in two layers of heavy-duty foil and place around the edges of the fire. After 20 to 30 minutes or so, depending on the vegetable, they will have an incredible, pure flavor that is almost indescribable. For a variation on the theme, add a few leaves of rosemary, summer savory, or sage and a drop or two of fragrant extra-virgin olive oil to each packet before roasting.

GRILLING YEAR-ROUND

Depending on where you live, you may be able to grill outdoors for most or all of the year. For those who live in cooler climates (and city dwellers without access to a grill when they're not on vacation), note that most of the recipes in this book can be cooked under the broiler or on a ridged grill pan on the stovetop. Timing may vary slightly—just follow the visual clues for doneness in the recipe, and adjust the cooking time as necessary.

EQUIPMENT

Once you've got your grill, you don't need a lot of special equipment, but there are a few things that will make grilling easier and more fun.

GRILL BRUSH A good grill brush is essential for keeping the grill clean. Choose a sturdy wire brush that will stand up to the job; one with brass bristles will not rust.

TONGS It's handy to have at least two pairs of long spring-loaded tongs for turning and moving foods on the grill; I have a couple of pairs of short tongs too.

BASTING BRUSHES You can buy long-handled basting brushes designed for grilling or just pick up a couple of natural-bristle (not nylon, which can melt) paintbrushes at the hardware store.

DRIP PANS Many gas grills come with their own metal drip pan, and you can buy disposable foil drip pans, to use in either a gas or a charcoal grill, at the hardware store. Foil loaf pans or small foil baking pans, available in any supermarket, also work fine in a charcoal grill.

SPATULA A long-handled wide spatula or pancake turner is handy for turning some grilled foods. Be sure it's metal, not plastic.

SKEWERS Wooden skewers are inexpensive and available in any supermarket; 12-inch-long skewers are best for grilling. Soak wooden skewers for at least 30 minutes before using them. Metal skewers come in various styles; flat ones are generally better than round ones because they help keep the food from flipping around as you turn the skewers.

SAFETY TIPS

Make sure the grill is on a level surface and away from overhanging tree branches, awnings, etc.—anything that could catch fire. Never grill in a garage or other enclosed space or in a poorly ventilated area, or you risk (deadly) carbon monoxide buildup.

As mentioned above, always open the lid of a gas grill before you turn on the fuel supply, and make sure all the burners have ignited before you close the lid for preheating. If using a chimney or electric coil starter for a charcoal grill, put it in a safe place to cool.

Keep a plastic spray bottle filled with water near the grill to deal with serious flare-ups. Char is good, incinerated is not. But don't soak the food or the fire—often just moving the food away from the flare-up or closing the grill lid (or turning off a gas burner for the moment) will do the trick. To help prevent flare-ups, be sure to trim excess fat from any food before grilling it. And keep a fire extinguisher on hand for emergencies.

Although larger cuts of meat (and anything that will be spit-roasted) should be brought to room temperature before grilling, don't overdo it—20 to 30 minutes should be enough time for most foods, 1 hour max for really big steaks or roasts. Fish should be kept refrigerated until just before cooking, as should any other highly perishable foods.

When marinating, don't allow the food to stand at room temperature for any longer than the time specified in the recipe; cover it and marinate it in the refrigerator if you aren't planning to cook it until later.

If you want to use a marinade for a sauce or serve it as a dipping sauce, you need to heat it, because it will have absorbed raw juices from the marinated meat or fish. Pour it into a saucepan, bring to a boil, and boil for 1 minute. If you are planning to serve some of the barbecue sauce or glaze you are using to baste the food as it grills, it's best to divide the sauce between two containers and use one for basting, one for serving. And, in most cases, wait until the surface of the meat or other food has seared and cooked before you start basting (this way, you avoid contaminating the basting brush—and remaining sauce). For barbecue sauces and glazes that contain sugar or another sweetener, you always want to wait until the food is almost cooked anyway, or the sauce will burn on the grill.

Never put cooked food back on the platter you used to bring it out to the grill. Put out a clean platter before you start grilling, when you aren't distracted by cooking.

When spit-roasting, remember that the spit will be very hot when you take it off the fire. Have someone help you do this if possible, and put the hot spit in a safe place so no one will touch it and get burned.

Finally, relax and have fun!

INGREDIENTS

AND TECHNIQUES FOR THE ITALIAN KITCHEN

ALMONDS In Italy, you will find two varieties of almonds: bitter and sweet. Bitter almonds, which contain a toxic acid when raw, are used to make almond extract and amaretto. Only sweet almonds are available in the United States. They can be found raw or roasted; blanched (skinned) or unblanched; salted or not; and whole, sliced, or slivered. They can also be ground into almond flour or used to make almond paste. Almonds should be purchased in the shell if possible; otherwise, select those packed in tightly sealed jars, cans, or bags.

ANCHOVIES These small flavorful fish from the Mediterranean and the southern Atlantic are eaten both fresh and preserved in salt or oil. In this country, we most often see the latter, flat or rolled fillets in oil, but the best anchovies are packed whole in salt. Salt-packed anchovies must be filleted and rinsed before they are used; in some recipes I call for soaking them in milk before using to remove more of the salt. The least desirable anchovies are made into anchovy paste, sold in tubes or sometimes in jars. In some recipes, the paste will do, but for superior flavor and sublime texture, salt-packed anchovies are the ones for me—and you.

ARTICHOKES To trim artichokes, remove the tough outer layers of leaves from each artichoke by snapping them off until you reach the pale yellow inner leaves (the larger the artichoke, the more layers you will have to remove). Cut off the top third of the artichoke leaves with a sharp knife. As you work, rub the cut surfaces of the artichoke with a lemon half to prevent oxidation (browning). Trim off the bottom of the artichoke stem and, using a paring knife, remove the tough outer layer from the stem. Using a grapefruit spoon or small sharp spoon, scrape out the fuzzy choke from the center of the artichoke. Pull out the small purple leaves. Put the artichokes in a bowl of lemon water until ready to cook.

Or, if you will be serving the artichokes whole, simply cut off the top third of each one and trim off the stems so the artichokes will stand upright. As you work, rub the cut surfaces with a lemon half to prevent oxidation. Pull off the smaller leaves around the bottom of each artichoke. Put the artichokes in a bowl of lemon water until ready to cook.

ARUGULA Also known as rucola, its Italian name, or rocket, arugula has long narrow leaves and a pleasing bite. Its flavor varies with both type and the season, so some bunches will be more pungent than others. There are several types you are likely to see in the market; I like them all. Some varieties have big thick leaves, others have smaller, more delicate leaves. Wild arugula has narrow leaves and a sharper taste. Baby arugula, with a delicate flavor, is becoming increasingly available. Arugula is quite perishable; store it wrapped in a damp paper towel in a plastic bag in the refrigerator for no more than a day or two.

BALSAMIC VINEGAR Real balsamic is a deep, intensely flavorful vinegar made exclusively in Emilia-Romagna from the unfermented juice of white Trebbiano grapes. The freshly pressed juice is cooked slowly overnight in copper cauldrons over open fires right in the vineyard, to form a thick syrup called *mosto* or *saba*. The mosto is put into giant wooden barrels and then aged in a series of successively smaller barrels of different woods over a period of twelve years or more to achieve balsamic vinegar's unique and complex flavor. The finished product must be submitted to a consortium for tasting, and if it is approved, it is poured into bottles whose shapes indicate the place of origin, either Modena or Reggio— the only two areas that can legitimately produce the real thing. True *aceto balsamico tradizionale* will cost you at least fifty dollars for a four-ounce bottle and should be used to dress salads only if you own the joint. The supermarket stuff sold in tall green bottles for $3.99 is a pale imitation of the true thing and contains caramel coloring. It's fine for a change of pace in the salad dressing department but unacceptable in the realm of anointing perfect meats, such as grilled rib eye (see page 170), or a chunk of Parmigiano-Reggiano, where you want the real thing.

BLACK PEPPER Some of the recipes in this book call for a large amount of pepper, several tablespoons or so. Even if you often use a spice (or coffee) grinder for spices like cumin or fennel seeds, you may never have thought of grinding pepper this way. The spice grinder

seems to release even more of the fragrant oils, and it's quick and easy when you need a lot of ground pepper. Pepper should always be freshly ground, whether in a pepper mill or a spice grinder, so it's best to grind just the amount the recipe calls for (though if you do have a bit left over, you can store it in a tightly sealed jar to use within a day or so).

BOTTARGA Once known as the poor man's caviar, bottarga is the salted, pressed, and dried roe of either tuna (*tonno*) or gray mullet (*mugine*). In Sicily and Sardinia, the tradition of preserving seafood is well maintained to this day. There the long, fat roe sacs are salted and massaged by hand over a period of several weeks to preserve them. Then the roe is pressed under wooden planks weighted with stones and sun-dried for one to two months. Both types are salty, but tuna bottarga has a lively, sharp flavor, stronger than mullet bottarga. Bottarga can be shaved, sliced, chopped, or grated, and just a little can add a lot of flavor to a whole range of dishes. I love a salad of bitter greens dressed with fresh orange juice, extra-virgin olive oil, and shaved bottarga (use a Microplane grater to shave the bottarga). Keep bottarga tightly wrapped in the freezer.

BREAD CRUMBS We use bread crumbs in various forms in many dishes at our restaurants, both for coating ingredients before sautéing or frying them and in stuffings for vegetables, meat, fish, and poultry. They also make a nice crust when browned atop a dish or toasted. To make fresh bread crumbs, just grind chunks or torn slices of bread to the desired size in a food processor. We use both finer crumbs and "fat boys"—crumbs that are about ¼ inch in size, which we usually toast, sometimes in a little oil. To toast fresh bread crumbs, spread them on a baking sheet and bake in a 300°F oven for about 12 to 15 minutes, stirring frequently, until golden brown. To make dried bread crumbs, dry chunks or slices of fresh bread (don't use stale bread) in a low oven, then break them up and process to crumbs of the desired size. Ready-made bread crumbs are available in the bakery department of some grocery stores and at specialty markets. The bread crumbs sold in canisters are unacceptable.

BRUSCHETTA AND CROSTINI Although the terms are sometimes used interchangeably here, *bruschetta* and *crostini* are actually different, though both are variations on a theme. The word *bruschetta* comes from *bruscare*, which means to cook over hot coals, and bruschetta (technically the plural is *bruschette*, but *bruschetta* has come to be used for both forms here) is grilled thick slices of country bread that are served warm, sometimes with no other adornment than a quick rub with a garlic clove and a drizzle of extra-virgin olive oil. Other traditional toppings include white beans seasoned with olive oil and herbs and chopped ripe tomatoes with basil. In some regions of Italy, bruschetta is called *fett'unta—fetta* means "sliced" and *unta* means "greasy," so *fett'unta* is a nice greased slice of bread. Crostini are more often made from long, thin loaves of bread, such as *filone*, and sliced thinner. They may be toasted or fried in olive oil, and they are usually served at room temperature, topped with anything from a savory chicken liver paste to a chunky olive puree.

CAPERS/CAPER BERRIES Capers are the flower buds of a creeping shrub called *Cappari spinosa* that resembles something from an exotic nursery. During their very short season, the unopened flower buds are picked daily just before they open. Capers may be preserved in a vinegary brine or in salt. Packed in brine, they lose much of their subtle flavor, but they will add a lot of magnificent acidity to your dish as a result of the formation of capric acid. I prefer capers packed in salt, which retain a sweet forest-floor flavor as well as the more subtle sea breeze scent that is lost in the pickling process. The best capers come from the island of Pantelleria, off the coast of Sicily. At the end of the season, the fruit of the caper bush develops into a drupe, or berry, that looks kind of like a small tomatillo. Sold pickled or salted, these make a great flourish for any dish with capers in it—and show off your super-savvy Mediterranean pantry.

CEPHALOPODS *Octopus*, like squid and cuttlefish, is a cephalopod, a class of mollusks. Octopi can grow to as long as fifty feet, but the ones you will see in the market are from two to three feet long. Smaller octopus is usually the most tender, but even so must be tenderized (see below). Baby octopi, no larger than two to three inches, are increasingly available, and they are very tender. An octopus has eight tentacles, and both the tentacles and the body are edible. Like squid, octopi have ink sacs, which, in the wild, can be used to create a liquid smoke screen to hide the octopus from its foe. In the kitchen, the ink can be used to color risotto or pasta.

Many fish markets sell octopus already cleaned, or you can ask the fishmonger to do it for you. Frozen octopus is fine—in fact, freezing helps tenderize it.

Tenderizing Octopus Many cooks dismiss octopus as rubbery, an unfortunate reputation bolstered by images of rugged fishermen squatting on the rocks by the sea and flailing away at the poor creatures. I've tried beating them with mallets, puncturing them all over with a fork, and marinating them with an acidic ingredient, but what really makes octopus tender is a wine cork. Cooking the octopus at a low boil with a cork in the water results in edible flesh in much less time, with much less of the toughness associated with OPC (other people's cephalopods). I've heard this is the result of an enzymatic reaction between something in the cork and the protein in the flesh, but beyond that I cannot say.

Calamari, or squid, can grow to as long as ninety feet, but the ones in the market are usually about six to eight inches long. They have ten tentacles, and both the bodies and the tentacles are eaten. Most fish markets now sell cleaned calamari. You can buy either bodies or tentacles, or a combination, depending on the recipe.

Calamari must be cooked either quickly or for a long time—nothing in between, or it will be disappointingly tough. Cook it for just a few minutes, or braise or stew it for 45 minutes or so. Squid ink can be used to color risotto or pasta.

Cuttlefish is related to squid, but its body is more oval and squat and the tentacles are shorter. From Mediterranean waters, cuttlefish are much more common in Italy than they are here, but you may be able to get them, fresh or frozen, at a good fish market. (If so, substitute them for the calamari in Calamari Spiedini in Lemon Leaves, page 88.) The ones in the market are about six to ten inches long, and they must be tenderized like octopus (see above). Cuttlefish also have an ink sac, though their ink is brown rather than black (the Italian name for cuttlefish is *séppia*, the origin of our word "sepia"); it can be used in cooking the same way as squid ink.

CHICKPEAS Also called ceci beans or garbanzos, these legumes, *Cicer arietinum*, are usually sold dried or canned. Like most dried beans, they must be soaked before cooking. Chickpea flour, ground from dried beans, is the main ingredient in *panissa*, a flat pancake served as both antipasto and bread in Liguria, and in the Sicilian *panelle*. Always buy dried beans from a market with a good turnover; the older they are, the harder they are to get just right when cooking.

CITRUS ZEST Citrus zest refers to the colored part of the peel of lemons and other citrus fruits, with none of the bitter underlying white pith. The easiest way to grate citrus zest is to use a Microplane rasp grater. A citrus zester is a small kitchen tool that removes the zest in thin strips; you can also remove the zest in strips using a vegetable peeler or sharp paring knife (be sure to remove any of the white pith from the strips), depending on how you will be using it.

FENNEL POLLEN Fennel pollen tastes like fennel seeds, only more so. It's a "secret ingredient" in Tuscan cooking, where it is used for cured meats and to season fish, chicken, and, especially, pork. Fennel pollen is harvested from wild fennel plants just as they begin to bloom, and it will transform almost anything you sprinkle it over. It's available in some specialty markets and can be ordered online (see Sources, page 232).

FREGOLA Fregola, also spelled fregula, is a Sardinian pasta made from durum semolina. It was traditionally formed into tiny balls by hand, then dried and toasted; today it is also commercially produced. Fregola is sometimes referred to as Sardinian couscous, but it's more flavorful and is slightly chewy. There's also a larger version, called fregolone. Fregola is available at some Italian markets and can be ordered online (see Sources, page 232).

GORGONZOLA This famous Italian blue cheese, named for the small town in Lombardy where it originated, is made from cow's milk that is inoculated with the *Penicillium gorgonzola* mold to produce the characteristic blue-green striations. Originally the mold was produced naturally by aging the cheese in damp caves where the mold grew, but today the cheese is injected with the mold and then aged for three to six months. Gorgonzola cheese is sometimes referred to as *erborinato*, "herbed" in Lombard dialect, because of its greenish striations. There are two types of Gorgonzola: *dolce* (meaning "sweet") is creamy and mild; *naturale* is aged longer, is firmer, and has a more pungent bite.

INSTANT YEAST Also called rapid-rise yeast, instant yeast is a quick-rising type of active dry yeast. It cuts rising times considerably, and it also has the advantage of not needing to be "proofed," or dissolved in liquid—it can simply be added to the other dry ingredients in the recipe. It is sold in foil-lined ¼-ounce envelopes, three to a pack, and can be found in the baking aisle of the supermarket.

JERUSALEM ARTICHOKES Also called sunchokes, Jerusalem artichokes are small pale brown tubers with sweet, slightly nutty-tasting flesh. Despite their name, they have nothing to do with either globe artichokes or Jersusalem. In fact, they are related to the sunflower, and it's likely that their name comes from *girasole*, the Italian word for that flower—despite the fact that they are actually a North American native. Look for Jerusalem artichokes at farmers' markets and specialty produce markets. Their season runs from fall into spring, although you may find them at other times of the year. Some varieties are very knobby, others are smooth—the smooth ones are easier to clean. They can be eaten raw or cooked, and it is not necessary to peel their thin skins (though you may choose to do so)—just scrub them well.

MALDON SALT Harvested along England's Atlantic coast, Maldon salt is a high-quality sea salt with a delicate briny taste. Look for it in gourmet markets or order it online (see Sources, page 232). I use it to finish the scallops on page 106 and other seafood dishes.

MICROPLANE GRATER The Microplane is a rasp grater that has made the task of zesting citrus fruit immeasurably less tedious. There are now many different versions of the original Microplane (and other brands as well); the basic cheese grater/zester is versatile enough for most jobs. At Babbo, we also use a Microplane to shave bottarga over a dish. Less clunky than a box grater and decidedly sexier, the rasp gives you more control in finishing a dish with Parmigiano or another cheese.

MOSTARDA *Mostarda di Cremona*, also called *mostarda di frutta*, is a condiment made of fruits preserved in a thick sweet syrup that is seasoned aggressively with ground mustard seed and other spices. It is a classic accompaniment to boiled meats in Lombardy and other parts of northern Italy. It can be found in Italian specialty markets or ordered online (see Sources, page 232).

MOZZARELLA Mozzarella is what is known as a pulled-curd cheese, *pasta filata* in Italian, because of the way it is made: big blocks of curd from either buffalo or cow's milk are cut into smaller pieces and soaked in hot water until the curd releases its liquid, the whey. Then the curd is kneaded by hand and stretched until it has reached the proper consistency. At exactly the right moment, the cheesemaker shapes the cheese by ripping off pieces (a technique known as *mozzando*, from the verb *mozzare*—thus mozzarella) and forming them into large or small balls. The smaller balls are called *bocconcini* or, sometimes, *ciliegini*, meaning "little cherries." Stretching and pulling the curd gives the cheese its characteristic slightly stringy consistency, resulting from the many layers that make up the final product. Originally produced almost exclusively in Campania and Sicily, *mozzarella di bufalo* is protected under DOP regulations; today it is also made in Basilicata and Calabria. Buffalo mozzarella has more flavor than mozzarella made with cow's milk; it is sweet with a slight tang and a creamy, milky bite. It is an essential part of the wood-fired *pizze* of Naples, and it is often served on its own, accompanied by a slice of grilled bread (bruschetta) and perhaps a simple salad. That said, some artisanal producers today are using cow's milk for their mozzarella, with slightly different but very good results. Fresh mozzarella may be salted or unsalted; it can also be smoked. Look for fresh mozzarella at an Italian or cheese market; avoid at all costs the rubbery slabs of domestic mozzarella in the supermarket.

OLIVE OIL The pressed extract of the fruit of the olive tree, olive oil is produced in nearly every province of Italy. Each has its own style and flavor, which in turn defines the style and flavor of the region's cooking. I recommend keeping two kinds of oil in the pantry: a boutique Tuscan or Ligurian extra-virgin olive oil, for anointing both raw and cooked foods at the moment they are served, and a less expensive extra-virgin oil from a larger producer—that is, a less distinctive but still high-quality oil, at a much lower price—for everything else, including frying and sautéing. That said, in my opinion, you simply cannot scrimp when buying extra-virgin olive oil. Choose one that you like for general use and stick with it, but from time to time, try other oils from other areas, particularly when cooking dishes from those regions. My personal favorites are Tenuta di Cappezana (western Tuscany), Castello di Ama (Chianti), and DaVero, produced by my friends Ridgely Evers and Colleen McGlynn in California's Dry Creek Valley from the fruits of trees transported from my grandfather's hometown of Segreminio, near Lucca. It has a rich and peppery intensity.

OLIVE PASTE This is a great convenience product that can be stirred into sauces and salad dressings, spread on crostini, and more. Made from either black or green olives, it is available in gourmet markets and some supermarkets.

OLIVES The fruit of the olive tree must be cured—and, in the process, preserved—using salt, water, lye, or oil, or a combination, before it is edible. Uncured olives contain a bitter component called glycoside that is leached out during the cure. All olives start green and eventually ripen to purple or black. Every olive-producing area in the world has its own variety of olives and seasoning profile, and I love them all. My favorites include Gaeta,

Kalamata, and Alfonso, but I am happy to try any I encounter. I cure my own each year for gifts to fellow olive *appassionati* and for the restaurants.

PANCETTA Pancetta, Italian bacon, is cured pork belly. In Italy it is available both rolled (*rotolata*) into cylinders and unrolled, or flat (*stesa*). Here you are most likely to find the rolled version, which the butcher will slice for you. If you are unable to find pancetta, artisanal-style American bacon, available in gourmet markets and some better supermarkets, makes an excellent substitute; www.gratefulpalate.com is a great online source for good bacon.

PARMIGIANO-REGGIANO Parmigiano-Reggiano is the undisputed king of cheeses, and its production is strictly regulated under DOC laws. In order to be considered true Parmigiano, the cheese must have been made entirely in a restricted area that includes the provinces of Parma, Modena, and Reggio-Emilia and parts of Bologna and Mantova. And the cheese is produced only from April to early November. The rind of true Parmigiano is always imprinted all over with the term "Parmigiano-Reggiano," verifying its authenticity. There are just six hundred or so dairies authorized to make it, following the traditional method: Two milkings from the dairy's cows (and/or those from nearby farms) are used for each batch, and it requires about 160 gallons of milk for each huge wheel of cheese; the average weight of a wheel of Parmigiano is 80 pounds. The milk from the evening milking is left to stand overnight before it is turned into curds; the morning milk is allowed to sit only briefly before it is turned into curds, and then the two are combined. The milk used

for the cheese is partially skimmed, as much of the cream is removed (and used for butter or another dairy product) before it is heated, fermented with some of the whey saved from the previous batch, and coagulated. The curd is then cut into tiny pieces and heated before it is finally wrapped in cloth and placed in large wooden molds. The cheese is left in the molds for several days, then it is soaked in a salty brine for about three weeks. Finally, it is aged for at least a year and for up to three or even four years before it is marketed.

Some Parmigiano enthusiasts claim to prefer cheeses made in the late spring and summer months, when the animals' feed is fresh grass and wheat. I like all of them, but I do prefer a younger cheese for eating unadorned or with balsamic vinegar and an older cheese for grating over my pasta and risotto.

PEPERONCINI Hot peppers are used mostly in southern Italy. The type varies from town to town, but the word *peperoncini* generally refers to the same crushed red chili flakes we find at the pizzeria. Most of us know our own preference for heat levels—I like a lot. I also like to use fresh chili peppers, especially the Mexican varieties like jalapeños, serranos, and sometimes even superhot habaneros, in many Italian dishes.

PIMENTÓN Pimentón is smoked Spanish paprika, and it's incredibly aromatic. The best comes from La Vera in Extramadura, and pimentón de la Vera is labeled *denominación de origen* (DO), signaling its unique status. There are three types of pimentón: *picante* (hot), *dulce* (sweet), and *agridulce* (bittersweet). Pimentón is available in many gourmet shops, or order it online (see Sources, page 232); La Chinata is one of the best brands.

PINE NUTS Pine nuts are the seeds from the pinecones of a stone pine, *Pinus pinea*. The best are the longer oval-shaped ones from the Mediterranean; try to get these rather than the more triangular-shaped variety from Asia. Because of their high oil content, pine nuts can turn rancid quickly. Store them in the freezer, and always taste one before adding the nuts to a dish.

POLENTA Polenta is the Italian version of cornmeal mush. It varies from region to region, in the way that the cornmeal is ground (coarse or fine), the way it is cooked, and the way it is served (soft and warm or cooled and set). Although I sometimes prefer the longer-cooking variety because its depth of rich corn flavor is unsurpassed, a good instant variety can be perfectly acceptable. Despite the "instant" on the package label, instant polenta is nothing like instant oatmeal or Minute rice. It's a pure product that contains nothing other than precooked cornmeal, and it can be very tasty indeed. And now that most brands seal the polenta in shrink-wrapped packaging, freshness (or lack of it) is no longer the issue it once was. Look for instant polenta in specialty markets and good supermarkets, or order it online (see Sources, page 232). I don't recommend cooking polenta in anything other than water (some cooks add milk), with a good amount of salt, because I prefer to let the simple, pure corn taste shine.

PORCINI POWDER Porcini powder imparts a deep, earthy fragrance to meats, stews, and other dishes. You can buy porcini powder at some gourmet markets and online, but we make our own at the restaurants by grinding dried porcini mushrooms very fine in a spice or coffee grinder. An ounce of dried porcini will yield about ¼ cup powder. Stored in a tightly sealed jar in a cool, dark place, porcini powder keeps almost indefinitely.

PROSCIUTTO Prosciutto is salt-cured, air-dried aged Italian ham. Until fairly recently, prosciutto di Parma, sometimes called Parma ham, was the only kind known here, but now several other excellent types are also imported. Prosciutto di Parma comes from Emilia-Romagna and is succulent and delicious. Prosciutto di San Daniele, from Friuli-Venezia, has a slightly sweeter taste. Prosciutto de Carpegna, from a small mountain town in Le Marche, is especially fragrant and delicate. Domestic prosciutto is an unacceptable substitute, so bite the bullet and splurge.

The most important tip is to buy your prosciutto from a shop that sells a lot of it—the less time that elapses after a ham is first cut into, the less chance it has to oxidize or dry out. The second most important tip is to have it sliced on a good machine and to have the butcher lay it carefully, not overlapping, on wax-coated paper, not parchment. Prosciutto does not hold well once it is sliced, even if done the right way, so buy just enough for a day or two—and return often to the shop, to help the prosciutto itself.

PROVOLONE Provolone, originally from southern Italy, is the Italian cheese with the greatest variety of shapes and weights, reflecting its ancient origins and deep roots. Each community that produces it has its own characteristic shape. The flavor becomes tangier and the texture flakier as the cheese ages. An excellent table cheese, provolone can be found in smoked versions as well. It is also a good cooking cheese because of its ability to stretch, melt, and flirt with other flavors in a dish. Be sure to buy Italian provolone, not the bland domestic version they slice at the deli.

RADICCHIO Radicchio, frisée, escarole, Belgian endive, and puntarelle, a favorite Italian green, are all members of the chicory (Chicorium) family. They all possess a somewhat bitter flavor that can be enjoyed raw or tamed with grilling or other cooking. There are two main types of radicchio. *Radicchio rosso* (red radicchio) includes the familiar round red heads found in most supermarkets, usually radicchio di Verona or radicchio di Chioggia. Radicchio di Treviso, which is increasingly available in gourmet markets and at farmers' markets, has a more elongated head, looking something like romaine lettuce, with deep red leaves and white stems. Radicchio di Castelfranco, found in some specialty markets, looks more like a head of lettuce, with tender pale yellow leaves that are speckled with red.

RICOTTA Fresh ricotta is not really a cheese, but a product of the cheese-making process. Its name means "recooked," and it refers to the fact that it is made from whey that is heated twice. The whey left over from the daily cheese making is heated until it forms curds that separate out and rise to the surface of the liquid. The curds are then drained, traditionally in rush baskets, and the result is ricotta. Italian ricotta is usually made from whey from sheep's or water buffalo milk (most American ricotta is made from cow's-milk whey). It has a mild, nutty, sweet flavor and a drier texture than typical American ricotta.

In Italy, fresh ricotta is sold by weight and comes wrapped in wax-coated paper. If possible, ask to taste fresh ricotta before purchasing it to make sure it's still fresh. If it feels prickly on your tongue or tastes sharp and/or fruity, it's not. For an easy way to make "homemade" ricotta, see page 44.

ROBIOLA There are two main types of robiola. Robiola di Piemonte is the name given to a category of soft creamy cheeses that may be made with cow's, goat's, or sheep's milk. These are rindless fresh cheeses that are allowed to age for about a week or so. Robiola di Piemonte is usually formed into cubes or disks and packaged in wax-coated paper. Robiola di Lombardia—rarely available here—has a reddish-brown rind and a much stronger flavor. The Piemonte is the type you want for the recipes in this book; look for it at a specialty market or good cheese shop.

SALT There are now dozens of brands of great salt on the market. I use sea salt from Sicily, both fine and coarse. I like the coarse salt, with its large, chunky grains, for finishing meat and fish, as well as for sprinking on focaccia and other flatbreads.

SCAMORZA Scamorza is a cow's-milk cheese that is similar to mozzarella, with a slightly chewier texture; it is available both smoked and unsmoked. Look for it at specialty cheese shops or Italian markets (or see Sources, page 232).

SEMOLINA Semolina is ground from durum wheat, a hard wheat high in protein. It comes in both coarse and fine grinds; fine semolina is sometimes referred to as semolina flour. Semolina is used to make pasta and a version of gnocchi; it is also used in some tortas and other desserts.

SHRIMP SIZES Shrimp are categorized by weight, using a system based on number of shrimp per pound: "U-12 shrimp," for example, means that it takes 12 at most of these huge shrimp to make a pound. However, the signs you see at the market do not always reflect this system, and one store's large shrimp is another one's medium. But the fishmonger should know the "count," shrimp per pound, so you can always ask him or her about their size. In general, the larger the shrimp, the more expensive they are. Peeled shrimp, of course, are always more expensive than unpeeled.

Super-colossal (U-12): 12 or fewer shrimp per pound
Colossal (U-15): 11 to 15 per pound
Extra-large: 16 to 20 per pound
Large: 21 to 30 per pound
Small: 36 to 40 per pound
Cocktail or salad: 41 or more per pound

TOMATOES A perfectly ripe tomato is a beautiful thing. Unfortunately, tomatoes need to ripen slowly under a hot sun, and they have a short season. So, although a fresh tomato sauce made with ripe tomatoes may be perfect in the summer, it is always better to use high-quality canned or packaged tomatoes during the off-season. I like two types: canned San Marzano tomatoes and Pomì, packaged in shelf-stable pint containers.

Pear-shaped San Marzano tomatoes are a type of Roma, or plum, tomato. The real thing is grown only in San Marzano, near Mount Vesuvius, outside Naples. They are available here in specialty markets and some supermarkets (check the label carefully to make sure they are real San Marzanos from Italy) or can be ordered through www.sanmarzano-imports.com. I recommend buying these canned tomatoes and crushing them by hand for sauces, rather than buying canned crushed tomatoes. If you can't find plain San Marzano tomatoes, buy the cans that include a basil leaf or two and discard the basil. Pomì tomatoes, sold in most grocery stores, are simply delicious. You can buy them either chopped or strained (pureed); I often use the strained tomatoes for topping a pizza when I don't have a homemade sauce on hand.

VIN COTTO *Vin cotto* translates as "cooked wine," and it is the cooked must of wine grapes; it is also known as *mosto cotto*. Its consistency falls somewhere between that of an aged balsamic vinegar and a syrup. The must is boiled and reduced to about one-fifth of its original volume. The syrup can be used at that point, or it may be aged in oak barrels, like wine, to develop more complexity. The result is a rich, smooth, syrupy liquid that can be enjoyed with both sweet and savory foods and used in a variety of dishes.

I

ANTIPASTI

The antipasto course sets the tone of the meal to follow, and an antipasto prepared on the grill is a great way to start a relaxed summer meal. (FYI, *antipasto* means "before the meal"—*il pasto*—not "before the pasta," as many people believe.) Or you could just set out an array of antipasti and call it the meal. You can mix and match these recipes, or you could choose one or two of these grilled antipasti and then serve them with other dishes that don't require any real work, such as a bowl of mixed olives or a platter of prosciutto di Parma.

Many of these recipes, like the Sicilian Marinated Zucchini with Ricotta and Bottarga and Grilled Vegetable Salad Capri-Style, feature vegetables at the height of their season. Others combine vegetables with some of my favorite pork products, such as Radicchio in Pancetta with Pears and Balsamic. Some, like Grilled Peppers with Anchovies, Capers, and Bread Crumbs, are my versions of classics, while others, like Fresh Robiola Wrapped in Mortadella, stray deliciously from tradition. Prosciutto with Grilled and Fresh Figs celebrates the arrival of that luscious fruit in the market, and the sublime Fennel with Sambuca and Grapefruit is a celebration in itself.

Any good meal depends on balance. Acidity, intensity, weight, and the sheer amount of food can all be in balance if you consider these a bit when planning the menu. Serving a relatively rich dish like Robiola Wrapped in Mortadella with an acidic one like Vegetable Salad Capri-Style makes sense—they go well together both in terms of a balanced palate and from a presentation point of view. Then again, you do not want to overthink this. It's summertime, and you are cooking for good friends.

These recipes are perfect for casual entertaining. Some of them can be made ahead and served at room temperature, and most of them can be prepared partially or almost completely in advance, with just a few minutes on the grill right before serving. For example, the polenta for the two very different grilled polenta recipes—one with robiola and scallions, the other flavored and colored with an herbal "Green" and topped with a pickled onion and escarole salad—can be cooked hours or even days ahead.

Also keep in mind that there are recipes for antipasti in the pizza chapter and that some of the dishes in the vegetable chapter make perfect antipasti.

PORTOBELLOS
WITH ARUGULA AND PARMIGIANO

SERVES 6

6 large portobello mushrooms, stems removed

¼ cup plus 2 tablespoons extra-virgin olive oil

1 teaspoon anchovy paste

2 tablespoons balsamic vinegar

½ teaspoon dried thyme, crumbled

Generous 4 cups trimmed arugula, washed and spun dry

Juice of ½ small lemon

Coarse sea salt and freshly ground black pepper

A 4-ounce chunk of Parmigiano-Reggiano for shaving

PREHEAT A GAS GRILL or prepare a fire in a charcoal grill.

Place the portobellos on the grill and cook, turning two or three times, until slightly softened, 5 to 8 minutes. Transfer to a platter, arranging the mushrooms gill side up.

In a small bowl, whisk together ¼ cup of the olive oil, the anchovy paste, vinegar, and thyme. Spoon the mixture evenly over the portobellos and let stand for 30 minutes.

In a large bowl, toss the arugula with the remaining 2 tablespoons olive oil and the lemon juice. Season with coarse sea salt and pepper.

Divide the arugula among six plates and top each with a mushroom. Using a vegetable peeler, shave the Parmigiano over the salads. Serve immediately.

This was one of the first dishes I put on the menu at my restaurant Pó … a long, long time ago. You can vary it by using different greens, such as spicy young watercress, or other cheeses, including sheep's-milk cheese, semi-soft or aged. The beauty of the dish lies in the seemingly incongruous marriage of anchovies and mushrooms: anchovies plus mushrooms equals steak.

PROSCIUTTO
WITH GRILLED AND FRESH FIGS

SERVES 6

18 fresh Black Mission figs, cut in half

6 ounces thinly sliced prosciutto di Parma

Generous 4 cups trimmed arugula, washed and spun dry

⅓ cup chopped fresh Italian parsley

2 teaspoons chopped fresh rosemary

3 tablespoons extra-virgin olive oil

2 tablespoons balsamic vinegar

PREHEAT A GAS GRILL or prepare a fire in a charcoal grill.

Place 18 of the fig halves cut side down on the grill and cook just until lightly browned, 2 to 3 minutes. Transfer to a large bowl and let cool.

Divide the prosciutto among six plates, arranging it artfully.

Add the remaining figs, the arugula, parsley, and rosemary to the grilled figs, then add the olive oil and vinegar and mix gently with your hands, so as not to break up the figs. Arrange the fig salad on the prosciutto and serve immediately.

Wait until you can get really ripe fresh figs to make this—and then make it as many times as you can before the season is over. Italians would never grill figs (they'd just serve them fresh), but the grill caramelizes the natural sugars in the fruit and makes them even more luscious. I leave half of them ungrilled for a nice contrast.

ASPARAGUS
WRAPPED IN PANCETTA WITH CITRONETTE

SERVES 6

2 pounds large asparagus (12 to 18 stalks per pound)

4 ounces thinly sliced pancetta

Grated zest and juice of 1 orange

2 teaspoons Dijon mustard

¼ cup extra-virgin olive oil

Kosher salt and freshly ground black pepper

1½ tablespoons finely chopped fresh thyme

Coarse sea salt

SNAP THE TOUGH BOTTOM STALKS off the asparagus. Unroll the slices of pancetta and lay them out on a work surface. Lay an asparagus spear on a slight diagonal across the bottom of one slice and roll it up, covering as much of the stalk as possible but leaving the tip visible. Place on a tray or small baking sheet and repeat with the remaining asparagus (if you are using jumbo asparagus, you may have a few slices of pancetta left over for another dish).

Cover and refrigerate for 1 hour (this rest will help the pancetta adhere to the asparagus).

Preheat a gas grill or prepare a fire in a charcoal grill.

In a small bowl, whisk together the orange zest, juice, and mustard. Continuing to whisk, slowly drizzle in the olive oil until emulsified and smooth. Season the citronette with salt and pepper, and set aside.

Place the asparagus on the grill and cook, turning occasionally, until it is just tender and the pancetta is crisped, about 4 to 6 minutes. If the pancetta browns too much before the asparagus is cooked, move the spears to a cooler part of the grill.

Whisk the citronette again, and pour half of it onto a serving platter. Sprinkle with half of the chopped thyme and pile the asparagus on top. Drizzle with the remaining citronette and sprinkle with the remaining thyme. Serve with a small bowl of coarse sea salt for dipping.

A classic room-temperature antipasto, here with pancetta substituting for the traditional prosciutto, is transformed on the grill. You could stick with prosciutto, or even substitute really good bacon—not a double-smoked one, though, or the smokiness will overpower the asparagus.

GRILLED SCAMORZA
WITH OLIO PICCANTE

SERVES 6

Three 8- to 12-ounce scamorza, cut lengthwise in half

Extra-virgin olive oil for brushing

¼ cup slivered best-quality sun-dried tomatoes

½ cup Olio Piccante

1 bunch marjoram

PREHEAT A GAS GRILL or prepare a fire in a charcoal grill.

Brush the cut sides of the scamorza with olive oil. Rub the grill with an oil-soaked towel or use a basting brush to oil it. Place the scamorza cut side down on the hottest part of the grill and cook just until it is beginning to soften and color lightly, 1 to 2 minutes. Carefully turn over and cook on the rounded side for a minute or two to warm the cheese.

Transfer to a platter, arranging the cheese cut side up. Sprinkle each one with a few slivers of sun-dried tomato and drizzle with a bit of the spicy oil. Scatter a few marjoram leaves over each cheese, and place the rest of the bunch in the center of the platter so your guests can pinch off a little more to sprinkle on as they like.

Grilling soft and semi-soft cheeses is an old Neapolitan tradition, one that hasn't quite caught on yet with Americans. It might seem as if the cheese would just melt all over the grill, but it doesn't—and it's great: soft, not-quite-oozing cheese with a subtle smoky flavor.

OLIO PICCANTE
(SPICY OIL)

MAKES ABOUT 1½ CUPS

2 cups extra-virgin olive oil

5 jalapeño peppers, coarsely chopped

½ cup hot red pepper flakes

1 tablespoon sweet paprika

IN A SMALL SAUCEPAN, combine the oil, jalapeños, pepper flakes, and paprika and bring just to a simmer over medium heat.

Pour the oil (and flavorings) into a heatproof bowl and let cool, then cover and refrigerate for at least 8 hours, or overnight.

Strain the oil and keep refrigerated until ready to use. It can be stored in the refrigerator in a tightly sealed jar for up to 10 days—no longer.

Note: This is great drizzled over grilled vegetables, seafood pastas, or pizza and grilled bread.

FRESH ROBIOLA
WRAPPED IN MORTADELLA

12 to 14 thin slices mortadella (about 8 ounces; see Note)

12 ounces fresh robiola (or substitute fresh goat cheese or fresh ricotta)

12 fresh basil leaves

3 cups young dandelion greens or other tender bitter greens

3 tablespoons extra-virgin olive oil

1 tablespoon red wine vinegar

Coarse sea salt

PREHEAT A GAS GRILL or prepare a fire in a charcoal grill.

Lay 12 slices of mortadella out on a work surface. Place 2 tablespoons of the cheese in the very center of each slice, shaping it loosely into a log running across the slice. Place a basil leaf on top of each mound of cheese. Fold the bottom of each slice over the cheese, then fold over the sides and roll the cheese up in the mortadella (like a burrito). Secure each one with a toothpick.

Place the mortadella packets seam side up on the hottest part of the grill and cook until lightly charred on the bottom, about 2 minutes. Turn over and repeat on the second side, about 2 minutes longer. Transfer to a platter.

In a medium bowl, toss the dandelion greens with the olive oil and then the vinegar. Season with coarse sea salt and pile the greens over the hot and delightful mortadella packets. Serve immediately.

Note: Try to get mortadella without pistachios; if the only mortadella you can buy does have nuts in it, some of them may fall out when it is sliced—if necessary, buy one or two extra slices and use them to patch any holes in the 12 slices you need for the recipe.

Mortadella is a big fat smoked Italian sausage with a delicate flavor. Make sure to get real Italian mortadella, which has only recently become available here, not the pallid domestic version. You won't find an antipasto like this in Italy, but the combination of the melting rich cheese and the pork sausage is amazing. Don't rush it: let the mortadella packages sit on the grill long enough to char—it's those really darkened porky bits that make it so good.

RADICCHIO

IN PANCETTA WITH PEARS AND BALSAMIC

MAKES 12 PIECES

- 6 heads Treviso radicchio (or substitute red/ Verona radicchio or Belgian endive)

  Kosher salt and freshly ground black pepper

  About ¼ cup extra-virgin olive oil

- 12 thin slices pancetta

- 2 Comice pears

  Good balsamic vinegar for drizzling

CUT THE HEADS OF RADICCHIO lengthwise in half and lay cut side up on the cutting board. Season with salt and pepper and drizzle each half with a bit of olive oil.

Unroll the slices of pancetta. Tightly wrap each radicchio half in a slice of pancetta. Place the radicchio on a plate and refrigerate for 20 minutes (this will help the pancetta adhere to the radicchio).

Prepare a gas or charcoal grill for indirect grilling.

Place the radicchio cut side down on the cooler part of the grill, with the stem ends toward the fire. Cook slowly for 10 to 15 minutes, turning once, until the radicchio softens and the tips of the leaves are golden brown.

Meanwhile, core the pears and slice into very thin wedges. Set aside.

Move the radicchio to the hot part of the grill and cook for about 1 minute, turning once, to crisp the pancetta. Be careful not to let the flames lick up too high; if the radicchio begins to char, remove it from the grill.

Arrange the radicchio cut side up on a platter and drizzle with balsamic vinegar. Lay a couple of slices of pear over each one and serve immediately.

Bitter chicories like radicchio and endive do well on the grill—let the tips of the leaves get a little brown, but don't char them. Cool sweet pears are a nice contrast to the crisp pancetta. You could substitute good bacon for the pancetta: this recipe might be just the reason you need to join Grateful Palate's Bacon-of-the-Month Club (see www.gratefulpalate.com).

GRILLED
VEGETABLE SALAD
CAPRI-STYLE

SERVES 6

¼ cup red wine vinegar

3 garlic cloves, minced

1 teaspoon dried oregano, crumbled

1 teaspoon ground cumin

1 teaspoon Colman's dry mustard

1 teaspoon hot red pepper flakes

½ cup extra-virgin olive oil

Grated zest and juice of 1 orange

2 small Asian or Italian eggplant

2 red bell peppers

2 yellow bell peppers

12 baby zucchini with flowers or 4 small zucchini

2 medium red onions

6 scallions

12 spears pencil asparagus

Kosher salt

12 fresh basil leaves, cut into chiffonade (thin slivers)

PREHEAT A GAS GRILL or prepare a fire in a charcoal grill.

In a small bowl, whisk together the vinegar, garlic, oregano, cumin, mustard, red pepper flakes, olive oil, and orange juice (reserve the zest for garnish). Set aside.

Cut the eggplant into ½-inch-thick slices. Cut the peppers into quarters and remove the cores and seeds. If using baby zucchini, cut them lengthwise in half. If using small zucchini, cut lengthwise into ¼-inch-thick slices (discard the first and last slice from each). Cut the onions into 6 or 8 wedges each. Trim the scallions. Snap off the tough bottom parts of the asparagus stalks.

Place the vegetables on two large baking sheets. Brush lightly with some of the red wine vinegar marinade and season lightly with salt. Place on the grill over medium-high to high heat (you will probably have to cook the vegetables in batches) and cook, turning once or twice, until tender and slightly charred on both sides: the eggplant will take about 8 to 10 minutes, the peppers 10 to 12 minutes, the zucchini 6 to 8 minutes, the onions and scallions 4 to 6 minutes, and the asparagus 5 to 7 minutes. Remove each vegetable from the grill as it is done and return to the baking sheets.

Cut the peppers crosswise in half. Arrange the vegetables decoratively on a large serving platter and drizzle with the remaining marinade. Sprinkle with the orange zest and basil. Serve warm or at room temperature.

This is a typical Italian way of preparing vegetables, but I first had it in a little restaurant called La Capannina on the Isle of Capri, and so I think of it as Capri-style. The vegetables listed here are merely guidelines—as always, the fresher and more seasonal, the better.

MARINATED ZUCCHINI
WITH RICOTTA AND BOTTARGA

SERVES 6

- 4 medium zucchini, preferably 2 yellow and 2 green
- ¼ cup red wine vinegar
- 1 teaspoon black olive paste
- 1 teaspoon dried oregano, crumbled
- 1 teaspoon celery seeds
- 1 teaspoon hot red pepper flakes
- ¾ cup extra-virgin olive oil
- 1 cup fresh ricotta
- 1 tablespoon freshly ground black pepper
- A small chunk of bottarga (see page 15) for grating
- 16 fresh mint leaves
- 2 serrano chilies, sliced into paper-thin rounds

PREHEAT A GAS GRILL or prepare a fire in a charcoal grill.

Using a mandoline or other vegetable slicer, slice the zucchini lengthwise into ⅛-inch-thick slices.

In a shallow bowl, whisk the vinegar, olive paste, oregano, celery seeds, red pepper flakes, and ½ cup of the olive oil together to form a loose (broken) vinaigrette. Dip each zucchini slice in the vinaigrette, drain off the excess, and place on a large baking sheet.

Working in batches, place the zucchini on the grill and cook, turning once, just until it is slightly softened and pale grill marks appear, about 1 minute on each side, then return to the baking sheet.

In a small bowl, combine the ricotta with the remaining ¼ cup olive oil, mixing well. Stir in the black pepper.

Arrange the zucchini slices on a large platter. Pour all of the remaining vinaigrette over them. Spoon the ricotta mixture into the center and grate a lot of bottarga over the whole thing. Tear the mint leaves and scatter them haphazardly over the zucchini, then scatter the chilies over. Serve at once, or within an hour.

There are a lot of great flavors playing off each other in this Sicilian dish, but the final result really depends on the quality of the ricotta. Yes, you can use supermarket ricotta and it will still be good, but if you can get real fresh ricotta, it will be unbelievable. And if you can't, you can make a version of fresh ricotta very easily at home; see the recipe that follows.

HOMEMADE RICOTTA

MAKES ABOUT 2 CUPS

2 quarts whole milk

1 pint half-and-half

Generous pinch of kosher salt, or to taste

¼ cup distilled white vinegar or strained fresh lemon juice

POUR THE MILK AND HALF-AND-HALF into a large enameled or stainless steel saucepan, add the salt, and bring to a full boil. Remove from the heat, add the vinegar, and stir until the mixture has separated into thick curds and a clear liquid (the whey).

Set a sieve over a large deep bowl and line it with a double layer of wet cheesecloth (or a damp paper towel). Pour the curds and whey into the sieve and allow to drain for 15 minutes (or up to 30 minutes if you want a firmer cheese).

Scrape the ricotta into a bowl. It is ready to serve, or it can be covered and refrigerated overnight.

Use this in the zucchini recipe, or serve it on its own with grilled bread, great extra-virgin olive oil, and coarse sea salt.

GRILLED PEPPERS

WITH ANCHOVIES, CAPERS, AND BREAD CRUMBS

SERVES 6

4 yellow bell peppers

4 red bell peppers

¼ cup plus 2 tablespoons extra-virgin olive oil

2 kirby cucumbers, thinly sliced

6 salt-packed anchovies, filleted and soaked in milk for 1 hour, or 12 oil-packed anchovy fillets, drained

2 tablespoons capers

4 garlic cloves, thinly sliced

1 teaspoon dried oregano, crumbled

1 teaspoon fresh thyme leaves

¼ cup red wine vinegar

¼ cup caper berries

½ cup toasted "fat boy" bread crumbs (see page 15)

PREHEAT A GAS GRILL or prepare a fire in a charcoal grill.

Rub the peppers all over with 2 tablespoons of the olive oil. Place on the hottest part of the grill and cook, turning regularly, until charred and blackened all over, 10 to 12 minutes. Place the peppers in a paper sack and seal tightly, or put them in a large bowl and cover tightly with plastic wrap. Allow to cool and steam for 10 minutes.

Peel the peppers, remove the cores and seeds, and cut into triangles about 1 inch wide and 2 inches long. Place the peppers in a large bowl and add the cucumbers, anchovies, capers, garlic, oregano, thyme, the remaining ¼ cup olive oil, and the vinegar and toss carefully to mix well without tearing the peppers or anchovies. Let stand for 30 minutes. (The peppers can be made ahead and refrigerated for as long as overnight.)

To serve, arrange the peppers on a platter, making sure there are anchovies and cucumbers visible on top. Scatter the caper berries over the peppers and dust with the toasted bread crumbs.

The classic seen on every antipasto table from Naples to Palermo—to Jersey City. Too often, of course, it's made with jarred roasted peppers. You could substitute those in a pinch, but it's so much better with peppers you have just grilled yourself. When you toss them together with all the rest of the ingredients, the result is explosive.

FENNEL
WITH SAMBUCA AND GRAPEFRUIT

SERVES 6

3 large female (round) fennel bulbs, trimmed, fronds reserved for garnish

¼ cup plus 2 tablespoons extra-virgin olive oil

4 garlic cloves, thinly sliced

3 salt-packed anchovies, filleted, rinsed, and finely chopped, or 6 oil-packed anchovy fillets, drained and finely chopped

¼ cup sambuca

2 tablespoons balsamic vinegar

1 grapefruit

¼ cup fresh tarragon leaves

BRING A LARGE POT of salted water to a boil. Drop in the fennel bulbs and cook until just tender all the way through, 15 to 20 minutes. Meanwhile, set up an ice bath. Drain the fennel and cool in the ice bath, then remove and drain on a kitchen towel for 5 minutes.

In a small bowl, mix ¼ cup of the olive oil, the garlic, anchovies, sambuca, and vinegar together. Cut the fennel bulbs in half and set cut side up in a baking dish. Stir the sambuca mixture again and spoon over the fennel, letting it run down between the layers. Cover and refrigerate for at least 30 minutes, or as long as overnight.

Preheat a gas grill or prepare a fire in a charcoal grill.

Zest the grapefruit; set the zest aside. Using a sharp knife, cut off the top and bottom of the grapefruit to expose the flesh. Stand it upright on a cutting board and slice off the skin and all of the bitter white pith, working from top to bottom and following the natural curve of the fruit. Carefully cut each segment away from the membranes, sliding the knife down either side to release it. Set aside.

Drain the fennel over a small bowl, scraping each bulb lightly with a fork to get as much of the marinade as possible, and place on a plate. Add any marinade in the baking dish to the bowl, then add the remaining 2 tablespoons olive oil and the tarragon. Set aside.

Place the fennel cut side down on the hottest part of the grill and cook for 10 minutes, or until nicely browned. Turn and cook for 10 more minutes, or until lightly browned.

Arrange the fennel bulbs cut side up on a platter. Scatter the grapefruit segments over and around them and sprinkle with the zest. Strew the reserved fennel fronds around, drizzle with the marinade, and serve.

Blanching fennel before grilling it makes it meltingly tender and succulent. Add sambuca and grapefruit, and it's a party waiting to happen.

EGGPLANT ROLLATINI
WITH GOAT CHEESE AND PESTO

SERVES 6

3 medium eggplant

¼ cup extra-virgin olive oil, plus about ⅓ cup for brushing

Kosher salt and freshly ground black pepper

1 cup soft fresh goat cheese, such as Coach Farm

½ cup Pesto (recipe follows)

¼ teaspoon freshly grated nutmeg

1 cup Basic Tomato Sauce (recipe follows)

Generous 2 tablespoons fresh marjoram leaves

PREHEAT A GAS GRILL or prepare a fire in a charcoal grill.

Trim the eggplant and cut lengthwise into ⅓-inch-thick slices, discarding the first and last slices from each one; you should have about 18 slices.

Lay the slices on a baking sheet and brush on both sides with olive oil. Place over the hottest part of the grill, in batches if necessary, and cook, turning once, until soft and golden brown, 3 to 5 minutes on each side; return the slices to the baking sheet as they are done.

Season the eggplant slices on both sides with salt and pepper and arrange the slices on a work surface with a narrow end of each slice toward you. In a small bowl, mix the goat cheese, pesto, and nutmeg until smooth and well blended. Season to taste with salt and pepper. Place about 1 tablespoon of the mixture on the narrow end of each slice of eggplant and roll up, not too tightly, like a jelly roll. Set aside.

Put the tomato sauce in a medium bowl and whisk in the remaining ¼ cup olive oil. Season with salt. Spoon the sauce onto a rimmed platter or small serving plates. Arrange the eggplant rolls seam side down in the sauce and sprinkle with the marjoram leaves.

You can serve the eggplant now, or refrigerate it for at least 1 hour, or overnight, to allow the flavors to marry. If you chill it, remove it from the refrigerator 30 minutes before serving to come to room temperature.

These little rolls also make an excellent sandwich filling for a late-night snack: put a whole roll in a hamburger bun, squish it a bit, and rock on! Be sure to use medium eggplant, so they won't be too seedy.

PESTO

MAKES ABOUT 1 CUP

3 garlic cloves

2 cups lightly packed fresh basil leaves

3 tablespoons pine nuts

   Generous pinch of kosher salt

½ cup plus 2 tablespoons extra-virgin olive oil

¼ cup freshly grated Parmigiano-Reggiano

3 tablespoons freshly grated pecorino romano

WITH THE MOTOR RUNNING, drop the the garlic into a food processor to chop it. Add the basil, pine nuts, and salt and pulse until the basil and nuts are coarsely chopped, then process until finely chopped. With the motor running, drizzle in the oil. Transfer to a small bowl and stir in the Parmigiano and pecorino. (The pesto can be stored in a tightly sealed jar, topped with a thin layer of extra-virgin olive oil, for several weeks in the refrigerator.)

BASIC TOMATO SAUCE

MAKES 4 CUPS

¼ cup extra-virgin olive oil

1 Spanish onion, cut into ¼-inch dice

4 garlic cloves, thinly sliced

½ medium carrot, finely shredded

3 tablespoons chopped fresh thyme

   Two 28-ounce cans whole tomatoes

   Kosher salt

IN A LARGE SAUCEPAN, heat the olive oil over medium heat. Add the onion and garlic and cook, stirring occasionally, until soft and light golden brown, 8 to 10 minutes. Add the carrot and thyme and cook, stirring, until the carrot is softened, about 5 minutes.

Add the tomatoes, with their juices, breaking up the tomatoes with your hands, and bring to a boil, stirring often. Lower the heat and simmer until the sauce is as thick as hot cereal, about 30 minutes. Season with salt and remove from the heat. (Once cool, the sauce can be refrigerated, tightly covered, for up to 1 week or frozen for up to 6 months.)

GRILLED POLENTA
WITH ROBIOLA AND SCALLIONS

MAKES 16 PIECES

- 2 tablespoons honey
- 2 teaspoons chopped fresh thyme
- 1 tablespoon kosher salt
- 1 cup instant polenta or fine cornmeal
- 16 scallions, trimmed
- 5 tablespoons extra-virgin olive oil
- Grated zest and juice of 1 lemon
- Kosher salt and freshly ground black pepper
- 8 ounces fresh robiola, at room temperature
- About 1 tablespoon sweet pimentón (Spanish smoked paprika)

BRING 3 CUPS WATER to a boil in a large saucepan. Stir in the honey, thyme, and salt. Whisking constantly, slowly pour in the polenta in a thin stream, then cook, whisking, until the polenta thickens and you can see the bottom of the pan as you whisk, about 3 to 5 minutes for instant polenta, slightly longer for cornmeal.

Immediately pour the polenta into an ungreased 9-by-13-inch baking pan, spreading it evenly with a spatula or the back of a wooden spoon. Let cool, then refrigerate for 30 minutes, or until set. (The polenta can be refrigerated, covered, for several days.)

Preheat a gas grill or prepare a fire in a charcoal grill.

Place the scallions over the hottest part of the grill and cook until wilted and just charred on the first side, 4 to 6 minutes. Turn over and cook until charred on the second side, about 3 to 5 minutes. Transfer to a plate and set aside.

Flip the polenta out onto a cutting board (if you used fine cornmeal, you may need to run a blunt knife around the sides of the pan to release it). Cut into 8 equal rectangles, then cut each rectangle into 2 triangles. Brush the triangles on both sides with 3 tablespoons of the oil and place on the hottest part of the grill. Cook until grill marks form on the first side, 3 to 4 minutes, or a bit longer if necessary—let it go long enough so you get nice char marks. Turn and repeat on the other side, then transfer the grilled triangles to a large platter.

In a small bowl, toss the grilled scallions with the remaining 2 tablespoons olive oil and then with the lemon zest and juice. Season with salt and pepper to taste.

Spread each polenta triangle with 1 tablespoon of the robiola, mounding it slightly. Arrange a coiled scallion on top of each triangle and sprinkle with the pimentón. Serve warm or at room temperature.

Look for creamy robiola, without a rind, at a cheese shop or Italian market. If you can't get it, substitute another creamy cheese—or even Boursin.

GRILLED POLENTA VERDE
WITH ESCAROLE AND PICKLED ONIONS

MAKES 15 PIECES

3 tablespoons honey

1½ tablespoons kosher salt, plus more to taste

1½ cups instant polenta or fine cornmeal

"Green" (page 57)

1 large red onion

½ cup red wine vinegar

¼ cup sugar

¼ cup ice water

¼ cup plus 3 tablespoons extra-virgin olive oil

Scant 1 cup freshly grated Parmigiano-Reggiano

Freshly ground black pepper

1 head young escarole, outer leaves removed and reserved for another use, small pale inner leaves separated, washed, and spun dry

BRING 4½ CUPS WATER TO A BOIL in a large saucepan. Stir in the honey and salt. Whisking constantly, slowly pour in the polenta in a thin stream, then cook, whisking, until the polenta thickens and you can see the bottom of the pan as you whisk, about 3 to 5 minutes for instant polenta, slightly longer for cornmeal. Add the "Green," whisking until well mixed.

Immediately pour the polenta into an ungreased 10-by-14-inch baking pan or lasagne pan, spreading it evenly with a spatula or the back of a wooden spoon. Let cool, then refrigerate for 30 minutes, or until set. (The polenta can be refrigerated, covered, for several days.)

Meanwhile, slice the onion into ⅛-inch-thick rounds. Put in a medium bowl, add the vinegar, sugar, and ice water, and stir and toss to mix. Refrigerate for 30 minutes, stirring and tossing two or three more times.

Preheat a gas grill or prepare a fire in a charcoal grill.

Flip the polenta out onto a cutting board (if you used fine cornmeal, you may need to run a blunt knife around the sides of the pan to release it). Using a 2½-inch round cutter, cut out 15 rounds of polenta. Brush the rounds on both sides with 3 tablespoons of the oil and place on the hottest part of the grill. Cook until grill marks form on the first side, about 3 to 4 minutes. Turn and repeat on the other side.

Transfer the grilled polenta to a large platter and sprinkle each round with 1 tablespoon of the grated Parmigiano.

Drain the red onions, reserving ¼ cup of the pickling liquid, and place in a large bowl. Add the reserved pickling liquid, the remaining ¼ cup oil, and salt and pepper to taste. Add the escarole and toss to mix.

To serve, arrange the rounds of warm polenta on a platter and place a few leaves of escarole and rings of pickled onion on top of each one.

Chilled sweet-sour onions, warm herb-flecked polenta with melting cheese, and tangy bitter greens all come together in a blast of flavors, textures, and temperatures. The onion pickle is like a quick version of *agrodolce*, the traditional tart-sweet sauce. You only need the tiny inner leaves of the head of escarole for this; save the outer leaves to braise in olive oil with garlic.

"GREEN"

MAKES ABOUT 1/3 CUP

Kosher salt

Greens from 4 scallions

1 bunch Italian parsley, leaves only

1 cup baby spinach

100 mg ascorbic acid (vitamin C), crushed

¼ cup olive oil

BRING 4 QUARTS WATER TO A BOIL in a medium pot and add 2 tablespoons salt. Set up an ice bath. Drop the scallions, parsley, and spinach into the boiling water, stir to immerse the greens, and cook until tender, about 1 minute. Drain, plunge into the ice bath, and chill until very cold.

Drain the greens well. A handful at a time, squeeze the greens between your palms until no more water comes out. Or wrap them in a clean old kitchen towel and wring them dry.

Put the greens in a food processor, add the ascorbic acid and olive oil, and puree until smooth. Store in an airtight container in the refrigerator for up to 2 weeks.

"Culinary chlorophyll" is a vegetable extract made by putting dark green vegetables through a complicated process involving grinding, soaking, steaming, and more. Our much easier recipe for "green" adds an herbal, vegetal flavor to polenta and gives it an attractive green-speckled look. The ascorbic acid (i.e., vitamin C—buy it at the drugstore) stabilizes the color, and we use "green" in a lot of other things too, such as dressings for beans and potatoes.

II

PIZZA AND FLATBREADS

Pizza is such an iconic food that you may never have thought of it as a flatbread. But it is, of course, and it is just one of the dozens of regional flatbreads made all over Italy, all of which have their own personal histories, many of them stretching back centuries. Pizza has its own myriad variations, from the emblematic *pizza alla napoletana* to *pizza rustica*, a stuffed savory pie, to *pizza pasquale*, a sweet Easter bread. And then, of course, one town's *pizza* is another one's *focaccia*.

The origins of pizza date back to Greek and Roman times, but most culinary historians credit Naples with developing, or at least popularizing, pizza as we know it today, and it was well established there by the eighteenth century. (Remember that tomatoes were not known in the Old World until after Columbus's voyages to the Americas, and they did not become the staple they are today until several centuries later.)

In the United States, we think of focaccia as a square or rectangular flatbread with a characteristic dimpled surface, but in Italy, *focaccie* were traditionally round. Now, though, you will find rectangular versions in Genoa, the home of focaccia, as well as throughout Liguria and the rest of the country. Toppings are simple, sometimes no more than a sprinkling of rosemary leaves and a generous drizzle of extra-virgin olive oil. *Focaccine*, a *focaccia* cousin, may take different shapes. The two recipes here make long, rectangular, slightly puffy flatbreads, which I like to split open and fill: see Focaccina with Roasted Garlic, Scallions, and Provolone and Focaccina with Coppa and Apricots.

Schiacciata is the Tuscan name for focaccia or pizza (the word comes from the verb *schiacciare*, meaning "to flatten" or "to smash"). They can be large or small rounds or rectangles. I shape the dough for the two included here—one with grapes and fennel seeds, the other with prosciutto and a side of melon—into rough rectangles and grill-bake them on a piastra.

Piadina, another rustic flatbread with a long history, comes from Romagna. Modern versions are leavened with baking powder rather than yeast, and, unlike pizza or focaccia dough, often contain lard or another fat. You can fold or wrap these little breads around a savory filling, traditionally sautéed greens or sausage, but sometimes I split them and stuff them with "fancy" ingredients—prosciutto and mascarpone, say—for a rather refined variation on their country ancestors.

WHITE BEAN BRUSCHETTA
WITH GRILLED RADICCHIO SALAD

SERVES 4

1 cup cooked cannellini beans, drained and rinsed if canned

¼ cup extra-virgin olive oil

¼ cup balsamic vinegar

½ teaspoon hot red pepper flakes

2 tablespoons fresh basil leaves cut into chiffonade (thin slivers)

1 garlic clove, thinly sliced

Kosher salt and freshly ground black pepper

2 large heads radicchio di Treviso, halved lengthwise

Four ¾-inch-thick slices Italian peasant bread

PREHEAT A GAS GRILL or prepare a fire in a charcoal grill.

In a medium bowl, gently stir together the beans, 2 tablespoons of the olive oil, 2 tablespoons of the balsamic vinegar, the red pepper flakes, basil, and garlic. Season with salt and pepper. Set aside.

Place the radicchio cut side down on the grill and cook, turning once, until wilted and lightly browned in spots, 2 to 3 minutes per side; if the radicchio starts to char, move it to a slightly cooler spot. While the radicchio cooks, grill the bread until lightly toasted on both sides; set aside on a plate.

When the radicchio is done, transfer to a cutting board. Cut each half lengthwise in half again, slice off the cores, and separate the leaves. Toss the leaves with the remaining 2 tablespoons oil and 2 tablespoons vinegar, and season to taste with salt and pepper.

Arrange the radicchio leaves on four plates, fanning them out like the fingers of a hand. Spoon the beans, including a generous amount of the juices, onto the grilled bread. Place the bruschetta in the center or just below the center of each salad and serve.

This was one of the most popular dishes I served at Pó, and I still love it. Radicchio di Treviso has longer, narrower heads than the more familiar round red Verona type; if you can't find it, substitute red radicchio di Verona. You can make the beans up to a day ahead, and in fact they will be even more flavorful that way; store them in the fridge and bring to room temperature before serving.

TOMATO, MOZZARELLA, AND BASIL
BRUSCHETTA

SERVES 4

1 pound ripe tomatoes, cut into ¼-inch dice

4 ounces fresh mozzarella, cut into ¼-inch dice

3 garlic cloves, thinly sliced

1 teaspoon dried oregano, crumbled

12 medium fresh basil leaves, cut into chiffonade (thin slivers)

1 teaspoon hot red pepper flakes

3 tablespoons extra-virgin olive oil

Kosher salt

Eight ¾-inch-thick slices Italian peasant bread

Coarse sea salt

PREHEAT A GAS GRILL or prepare a fire in a charcoal grill.

In a medium bowl, combine the tomatoes, mozzarella, garlic, oregano, basil, red pepper flakes, and olive oil and toss or stir gently to mix. Season lightly with kosher salt and mix gently again. Set aside.

Grill the bread until dark golden brown lines form on the first side, 1 to 2 minutes, then turn over and repeat on the second side.

Arrange the grilled bread on a platter, top with the tomato mixture, and sprinkle with coarse sea salt. Serve immediately.

The whole game here is the quality of the mozzarella and the quality of the tomatoes—wait for summer. Best, of course, are vine-ripened tomatoes you have just picked yourself.

TUSCAN-STYLE CROSTINI WITH
CHICKEN LIVERS

SERVES 4 AS AN ANTIPASTO

3 tablespoons extra-virgin olive oil

1 small red onion, cut into ⅛-inch dice

8 ounces chicken livers, rinsed and trimmed

2 tablespoons capers

3 anchovy fillets, preferably from salt-packed anchovies, soaked for 1 hour in milk if salt-packed

1 teaspoon hot red pepper flakes, or to taste

½ cup dry white wine

Kosher salt and freshly ground black pepper

Twelve ¼-inch-thick slices thin Italian bread, such as *filone*, or baguette

PREHEAT A GAS GRILL or prepare a fire in a charcoal grill.

In a 10- to 12-inch sauté pan, heat the olive oil over medium heat. Add the onion and cook, stirring occasionally, until softened but not browned, about 6 minutes. Add the livers, capers, anchovies, and red pepper flakes and cook, stirring occasionally, until the livers are lightly browned, about 10 minutes. Add the wine and cook until it has evaporated, about 4 minutes.

Transfer the mixture to a food processor and pulse eight or nine times (quick 1- to 2-second blasts) just to a chunky puree, not until smooth. Season with salt and pepper and transfer to a bowl. (This keeps well, tightly covered, in the refrigerator for up to 4 days.)

Grill the bread, turning once, until deep golden brown on both sides, 1 to 2 minutes. Smear each toast with a generous tablespoon of the liver mixture and serve.

A classic Tuscan antipasto, made with chicken livers—or the livers of whatever bird you are cooking, such as guinea hen (see page 147). You can make the chicken liver topping well in advance, then just toast the bread when you fire up the grill for dinner.

PIZZA DOUGH

MAKES ABOUT 1¾ POUNDS

3¼ cups all-purpose flour, plus extra for dusting

2 teaspoons instant or rapid-rise yeast

1 tablespoon salt

1 tablespoon sugar

1 cup warm water

¼ cup dry white wine, at room temperature

2 tablespoons plus 1 teaspoon extra-virgin olive oil

IN A LARGE BOWL, combine the flour, yeast, salt, and sugar and mix well. Make a well in the center of the dry ingredients and add the warm water, wine, and olive oil. Using a wooden spoon, stir the wet ingredients into the dry until the mixture is too stiff to stir, then mix with your hands in the bowl until the dough comes together and pulls away from the sides of the bowl.

Lightly dust a work surface with flour and turn the dough out. Knead gently, dusting the work surface lightly with more flour as necessary, for 5 minutes, or until the dough is smooth, elastic, and only slightly sticky.

Oil a large clean bowl, add the dough, and turn to coat. Cover the bowl with plastic wrap or a kitchen towel, set in a warm part of the kitchen, and let the dough rise until doubled in size, about 1 hour.

Punch down the dough, and it is ready to use.

This is an easy and versatile dough. I use the same basic dough for many flatbreads, including the Sage Flatbreads on page 149, as well as pizza.

PIZZA MARGHERITA

MAKES 4 PIZZAS

Pizza Dough (page 66)

1 cup simple tomato sauce (I like Pomì strained tomatoes)

8 ounces fresh mozzarella, thinly sliced

About ¼ cup extra-virgin olive oil

24 fresh basil leaves

Coarse sea salt

PREPARE A GAS OR CHARCOAL GRILL for indirect grilling. For an even crisper crust, put a piastra (see page 9) on the hottest part of the grill to preheat.

Divide the dough into 4 pieces and shape each one into a ball. Let rest for 15 minutes, loosely covered with a tea towel or plastic wrap.

Using a floured rolling pin or your hands, stretch each ball into a 9- to 10-inch round (the shape doesn't have to be perfect).

Carefully lay one round of dough on the piastra or over the hottest part of the grill and cook until the bottom is lightly browned and dry, about 2 minutes. Using tongs, gently lift up the dough, flip over, and cook for just 30 seconds. Transfer to a baking sheet, with the less cooked side up, and repeat with the remaining dough rounds. Let cool.

Divide the sauce among the partially cooked pizzas and, using the back of a kitchen spoon, spread it evenly to within ½ inch of the edges of the dough. Divide the cheese among the pizzas.

Place 1 or 2 pizzas at a time on the cooler part of the grill and cook until the cheese is melted and the bottoms are crisp and golden brown, about 2 minutes. Transfer to a cutting board and drizzle with a little olive oil. Scatter 6 torn basil leaves over each pizza and sprinkle with coarse sea salt. Cut into slices with a pizza wheel and serve hot.

The quintessential pizza, named for Italy's Queen Margherita and sporting the colors of the Italian flag. Don't worry if the pizzas aren't perfectly round—in fact, they will look much more appealing if they are not. But be sure to let the dough set and firm up on the grill before flipping it over, or it may stick or tear. I once rushed this step on a live taping of *Good Morning America*, with disastrous results, so wait . . . just wait!

PIZZA
WITH HOT SALAMI AND PECORINO

MAKES 4 PIZZAS

Pizza Dough (page 66)

1 cup simple tomato sauce (I like Pomì strained tomatoes)

½ cup freshly grated pecorino romano

4 ounces thinly sliced spicy salami or pepperoni

About 2 tablespoons fresh marjoram or oregano leaves

PREPARE A GAS OR CHARCOAL GRILL for indirect grilling. For an even crisper crust, put a piastra (see page 9) on the hottest part of the grill to preheat.

Divide the dough into 4 pieces and shape each one into a ball. Let rest for 15 minutes, loosely covered with a tea towel or plastic wrap.

Using a floured rolling pin or your hands, stretch each ball into a 9- to 10-inch round (the shape doesn't have to be perfect).

Carefully lay one round of dough on the piastra or over the hottest part of the grill and cook until the bottom is lightly browned and dry, about 2 minutes. Using tongs, gently lift up the dough, flip over, and cook for just 30 seconds. Transfer to a baking sheet, with the less cooked side up, and repeat with the remaining dough. Let cool.

Divide the sauce among the partially cooked pizzas and, using the back of a kitchen spoon, spread it evenly to within ½ inch of the edges of the dough. Divide the cheese among the pizzas and arrange the salami on top.

Place 1 or 2 pizzas at a time on the cooler part of the grill and cook until the cheese is melted and the bottoms are crisp and golden brown. Transfer to a cutting board and sprinkle each pizza with one-quarter of the marjoram. Cut into slices with a pizza wheel and serve hot.

If you can, buy good imported salami or pepperoni; it will have much more character than the supermarket versions. Obviously my dad's—available through www.salumicuredmeats.com—is the ultimate.

FOCACCINA

WITH ROASTED GARLIC, SCALLIONS, AND PROVOLONE

SERVES 6 AS AN ANTIPASTO

Pizza Dough (page 66)

½ to ⅔ cup roasted garlic paste (see sidebar)

2 cups grated young or semi-soft provolone

1½ tablespoons chopped fresh rosemary

1 bunch scallions, thinly sliced

PREHEAT A GAS GRILL or prepare a fire in a charcoal grill.

Divide the dough into 2 pieces. Using a floured rolling pin, roll each piece out to a rough rectangular shape about 12 inches long, 6 to 7 inches wide, and ¼ inch thick.

Carefully place one piece of dough on the hottest part of the grill. Cook until the bottom is light golden brown, about 2 minutes. Use tongs or a spatula to flip the dough over and cook on the other side in the same way. Transfer to a cutting board and let stand for 2 minutes. Repeat with the second piece of dough.

Use a serrated knife to cut each focaccina horizontally in half: hold the top of the bread with your non-cutting hand, maintaining consistent pressure as you cut it into two even halves. Smear the garlic paste over the top halves of the bread and divide the provolone between the bottoms. Sprinkle the rosemary over the garlic halves, and sprinkle the scallions over the cheese halves. Close the focaccine and wrap each one tightly in foil. Grill the sammies, turning once, until they are hot and the cheese is melting, 5 to 6 minutes. Unwrap, cut into 1½-inch-wide strips with the serrated knife, and serve.

ROASTED GARLIC

Roasted garlic is delicious, mild and almost sweet. Choose large heads with big, plump cloves; smaller heads with small cloves are tedious to deal with. A very large head will yield 3 to 4 tablespoons roasted garlic puree.

To roast garlic, preheat the oven to 350°F. Slice off the top ⅓ inch or so of each garlic head, exposing the cloves. Wrap the garlic heads individually in foil and roast for about 1 hour, until the cloves are very soft. Let cool, still wrapped in the foil, then remove from the foil and squeeze out the soft garlic from the skins and put it in a bowl. Using a fork, mash the garlic to a puree. (The garlic puree can be covered and refrigerated for up to 1 day; bring to room temperature before using.)

Same dough as the pizzas, but a different format. Each bread is made from half the dough, rather than just a quarter, so it is thicker, enabling you to split the focaccine for sammies.

FOCACCINA
WITH COPPA AND APRICOTS

SERVES 6 AS AN ANTIPASTO

Pizza Dough (page 66)

8 ounces thinly sliced coppa

1 cup fresh ricotta

1 pound apricots, pitted and sliced very thin

Freshly ground black pepper

PREHEAT A GAS GRILL or prepare a fire in a charcoal grill.

Divide the dough into 2 pieces. Using a floured rolling pin, roll each piece out to a rough rectangular shape about 12 inches long, 6 to 7 inches wide, and ¼ inch thick.

Carefully place one rectangle of dough on the hottest part of the grill and cook until the bottom is light golden brown and dry, about 2 minutes. Use tongs or a spatula to carefully flip the dough over and cook on the other side in the same way. Transfer to a cutting board and allow to stand for 2 minutes. Repeat with the second piece of dough.

Use a serrated knife to cut each focaccina horizontally in half: Hold the top of the bread with your non-cutting hand, maintaining consistent pressure as you carefully cut it into two even halves. Divide the coppa between the top halves and press down gently so it sticks. Spread the ricotta over the bottom halves, then divide the apricots between the ricotta halves, pressing them gently into the ricotta. Grind black pepper over the apricot sides. Close the focaccine and wrap each one tightly in foil.

Place the sammies on the grill and heat, turning once, until heated through, 5 to 6 minutes. Carefully unwrap, cut into 1½-inch-wide strips with the serrated knife, and serve.

Try this when you are lucky enough to come across—or pick—ripe, fragrant apricots. The apricots I get in Michigan in the summer are unbelievable, as juicy as a peach.

SCHIACCIATA

WITH CONCORD GRAPES AND FENNEL SEEDS

SERVES 6 AS AN ANTIPASTO

Pizza Dough (page 66)

¼ cup extra-virgin olive oil

2 cups Concord grapes, halved and seeded

¼ cup fennel seeds

Coarse sea salt

PREHEAT A GAS GRILL or prepare a fire in a charcoal grill. Put a piastra (see page 9) on the grill to preheat.

Divide the dough into 2 pieces. Using a floured rolling pin, roll each piece out to a rectangular shape about 12 inches long, 6 to 7 inches wide, and ¼ inch thick.

Carefully place one rectangle on the piastra (or cook both breads at the same time if your piastra is big enough) and cook for just 30 seconds. Carefully turn over and cook until the bottom is light golden brown and dry, about 1 minute. Transfer to a cutting board (with the less cooked side up), and repeat with the second piece of dough.

Brush the top of each bread with 2 tablespoons of the olive oil. Arrange the grape halves cut side down on the breads, using your fingertips to press them firmly into the soft dough. Sprinkle with the fennel seeds and sea salt. Using a large spatula, carefully place one of the breads (or both if you have room) on the piastra, cover with a large upside-down roasting pan, and cook, undisturbed, for about 5 minutes, or until the bottom is a deep golden brown and the top has cooked through; the grapes will be just starting to wilt. Transfer to a cutting board and repeat with the second bread.

Allow the schiacciate to rest for 5 minutes, then cut into wedges and serve.

Schiacciata with grapes is traditionally made to celebrate the grape harvest in Tuscany. If you can't get Concord grapes, you can use any grapes, even delicate little champagne grapes (which, by the way, are not related to Champagne—they are called that simply because they are so delicate and delicious).

SCHIACCIATA
WITH PROSCIUTTO AND MELON

SERVES 6 AS AN ANTIPASTO

Pizza Dough (page 66)

¼ cup extra-virgin olive oil

4 ounces thinly sliced prosciutto di Parma

1 small or ½ large ripe cantaloupe, seeded and cut into 6 wedges

PREHEAT A GAS GRILL or prepare a fire in a charcoal grill. Put a piastra (see page 9) on the grill to preheat.

Divide the dough into 2 pieces. Using a floured rolling pin, roll each piece out to a rectangular shape about 12 inches long, 6 to 7 inches wide, and ¼ inch thick.

Carefully place one rectangle on the piastra (or cook both breads at the same time if your piastra is big enough) and cook for just 30 seconds. Carefully turn over and cook until the bottom is light golden brown and dry, about 1 minute. Transfer to a cutting board (with the less cooked side up), and repeat with the second piece of dough.

Brush the top of each bread with 2 tablespoons of the olive oil. Divide the prosciutto between the breads, covering as much of the bread as possible. Using a large spatula, carefully place one of the breads (or both if you have room) on the piastra, cover with a large upside-down roasting pan, and cook, undisturbed, for about 5 minutes, or until the bottom is a deep golden brown and the top has cooked through. Transfer to a cutting board and repeat with the second bread.

Allow the schiacciate to rest for 2 minutes, then cut into squares or wedges, place on plates, and set a wedge of melon alongside each one.

Prosciutto and melon is a familar combination, but here the prosciutto melts on top of the grilled bread and the cantaloupe is served alongside for a cool contrast.

PIADINA DOUGH

MAKES ABOUT 2 POUNDS

4¼ cups cake flour, plus extra for dusting

1 tablespoon baking powder

1 teaspoon salt

⅔ cup lard or vegetable shortening, cut into tablespoons and chilled

1 cup ice water

COMBINE THE FLOUR, baking powder, and salt in a food processor and zap to mix. Scatter the pieces of lard over the flour and pulse just until incorporated. With the motor running, add the water and process just until the dough begins to clump together.

Turn the dough out and press it into a ball. It is ready to be used.

This dough uses baking powder rather than yeast for leavening. If you can get high-quality lard, do try it—lard always makes the best pastry and dough.

PIADINA
WITH PROSCIUTTO AND MASCARPONE

MAKES 12 SAMMIES

Piadina Dough (opposite)

12 thin slices prosciutto di Parma

1½ cups (12 ounces) mascarpone

PREHEAT A GAS GRILL or prepare a fire in a charcoal grill. Place a piastra (see page 9) on the grill to preheat.

Cut the dough into 12 pieces. On a lightly floured surface, using a lightly floured rolling pin, roll each piece into a 6-inch round, and place on two baking sheets or trays.

Working in batches, place the rounds on the piastra and cook until light golden brown on the first side, about 1 to 2 minutes. Turn and repeat on the other side. Transfer to the baking sheets.

When all are done, slice each round horizontally in half with a serrated knife: Hold the round with your non-cutting hand as you carefully cut it into two even halves. Place a slice of prosciutto on the bottom half of each one and smear 2 tablespoons of the mascarpone on the other half. Replace the top halves and press gently together.

Place the piadine on the grill for a minute or two to rewarm them, then wrap in a napkin and serve.

Piadine are a favorite snack in Romagna, the eastern part of Emilia-Romagna, where you will find them in every panini bar. Traditionally they were cooked on special embossed tiles, which imprinted them with a decorative pattern.

PIADINA

WITH TALEGGIO, COPPA, AND APPLES

MAKES 12 PIADINE

Piadina Dough (page 80)

2 Granny Smith apples

½ lemon

1 pound ripe Taleggio, at room temperature

8 ounces thinly sliced coppa

PREHEAT A GAS GRILL or prepare a fire in a charcoal grill. Place a piastra (see page 9) on the grill to preheat.

Cut the dough into 12 pieces. On a lightly floured surface, using a lightly floured rolling pin, roll each piece into a 6-inch round, and place on two baking sheets or trays.

Quarter the apples, core them, and, using a mandoline or other vegetable slicer, cut them into paper-thin slices. Put them in a shallow bowl and squeeze a little lemon juice over them, tossing gently so the slices don't break (don't worry if a couple of them do). Set aside.

Working in batches, place the rounds on the piastra and cook until light golden brown on the first side, about 1 to 2 minutes. Turn and repeat on the other side. Transfer to the baking sheets.

When all are done, smear the soft Taleggio evenly over the piadine and cover with the sliced coppa. Pile the apples on top of the coppa.

Place the piadine on the grill for a minute or two to rewarm them, then serve.

Taleggio is a creamy Italian cow's-milk cheese with a slightly nutty flavor. You could substitute Teleme from California, a creamy Fontina, or even Bel Paese, which has a similar texture.

III

FISH AND SHELLFISH

In Italy, cooking fish is all about freshness and simplicity—as I've said before, the philosophy of Italian fish cookery can be summed up in three words: *Leave it alone*. Complicated sauces and techniques are not part of the repertoire, and, in fact, Italians almost never serve any sauce at all with fish, other than an excellent olive oil. Lemon may sometimes appear, but even that is often considered beside the point. The one exception is *salsa verde*, the fragrant green herb sauce, which may sometimes accompany a fish with character enough to stand up to it, such as a whole grilled branzino (see page 126).

Few Italians would consider cooking anything other than local fish, whether from a mountain stream or the ocean, and I urge you to think in the same way: find a good fish market, and remember that what is freshest is best. If the specific fish called for in your recipe is not available—or doesn't look pristine and glistening—the fishmonger can help you choose another option (I include suggestions for substitutions in many of the recipes). If you are able to get fresh king mackerel for Mackerel "in Scapece" with Amalfi Lemon Salad, you will have the best mackerel dish you've ever tasted; if you can't find it, make the recipe with very fresh bluefish, or move on to another one. Most of the other fish recipes in this chapter, such as Monkfish in Prosciutto with Pesto Fregola and Swordfish Involtini Sicilian-Style, call for widely available varieties. But you'll want to be sure to get the best tuna available—sushi-quality, that is—for Tuna Like Fiorentina, and you really should use wild salmon for the Salmon in Cartoccio with Asparagus, Citrus, and Mint.

Cooking shellfish on the grill is easy, and the recipes in this chapter use several different techniques for achieving simple perfection. Clams *in Cartoccio* are wrapped in a foil package and allowed to steam in their fragrant juices. The shrimp in Shrimp Rosemary Spiedini alla Romagnola are threaded onto rosemary skewers, which impart their herbal fragrance and look sexy besides. I love cooking shellfish (and cephalopods) on a piastra, a flat griddle or stone placed on the hot grill (see page 9 for more on the subject), because it gives them a great sear and char, as in Sea Scallops *alla Caprese* or Marinated Calamari with Chickpeas, Olive Pesto, and Oranges.

Thinking globally while buying locally is especially important when you are buying fish. Some "trendy" fish have been overharvested to the point of extinction, and we now know that there can be problems with farmed fish as well, like salmon. The Monterey Bay Aquarium, at www.monterybayaquarium.com, maintains an up-to-date list of species that are being overfished in the United States and in the rest of the world. It's an invaluable resource, and I urge you to consult it when writing your shopping list, as I do both at home and at the restaurants.

CALAMARI
SPIEDINI IN LEMON LEAVES

SERVES 6

2 pounds cleaned calamari (bodies and tentacles)

½ cup extra-virgin olive oil, plus extra for serving

2 scallions, thinly sliced

3 garlic cloves, thinly sliced

1 tablespoon chopped fresh marjoram

2 teaspoons freshly ground black pepper

4 lemons, preferably Meyer lemons

36 whole lemon leaves or fresh Kaffir lime leaves or 18 fresh bay leaves, cut lengthwise in half

Kosher salt

Coarse sea salt

CUT THE CALAMARI BODIES crosswise in half if large. Split the groups of tentacles into 2 pieces each.

In a medium bowl, combine the olive oil, scallions, garlic, marjoram, and pepper, mixing well. Add the calamari and stir to coat. Cover and marinate in the refrigerator for 1 hour.

Cut 3 of the lemons into thin slices; you will need 36 slices. Cut the remaining lemon into wedges. Set aside.

If using wooden skewers, soak them in water for at least 30 minutes. Preheat a gas grill or prepare a fire in a charcoal grill.

Meanwhile, transfer the calamari to a plate; reserve the marinade. Assemble 12 spiedini, using both bodies and tentacles on each one and alternating the calamari with 3 lemon leaves and 3 lemon slices per skewer. Season aggressively with kosher salt and place on a rimmed platter. Pour the marinade over and place in the refrigerator for 10 minutes.

Place the skewers on the hottest part of the grill and cook, unmoved, for 6 minutes. Using tongs, gently turn them over and cook for 4 to 6 minutes more, or until the edges of the calamari are crisp and golden brown.

Serve on the skewers, with olive oil for drizzling, coarse sea salt, and the lemon wedges.

I originally had these spiedini in Positano, where they were made with scallops and big shrimp. The flavor the lemon leaves impart is incredible, an intensely fragrant burnt sweetness, with almost a campfire aroma. If you don't have a lemon tree in your backyard, unsprayed lemon leaves are sometimes available from florists; if you can't find unsprayed leaves, you can substitute fresh bay leaves or Kaffir lime leaves (see Sources, page 232; there are about 20 lime leaves in a 15-gram package).

MARINATED CALAMARI

WITH CHICKPEAS, OLIVE PESTO, AND ORANGES

SERVES 6

CALAMARI

3 pounds cleaned calamari (tubes and tentacles)

¼ cup extra-virgin olive oil

Grated zest and juice of 1 lemon

4 garlic cloves, thinly sliced

2 tablespoons chopped fresh mint

2 tablespoons hot red pepper flakes

2 tablespoons freshly ground black pepper

CHICKPEAS

Two 15-ounce cans chickpeas, drained and rinsed, or 3½ cups cooked chickpeas

½ cup extra-virgin olive oil

¼ cup red wine vinegar

4 scallions, thinly sliced

4 garlic cloves, thinly sliced

¼ cup mustard seeds

Kosher salt and freshly ground black pepper

OLIVE PESTO

¼ cup extra-virgin olive oil

Grated zest and juice of 1 orange

½ cup black olive paste

4 jalapeños, finely chopped

12 fresh basil leaves, cut into chiffonade (thin slivers)

3 oranges

2 tablespoons chopped fresh mint

CUT THE CALAMARI BODIES crosswise in half if large. Split the groups of tentacles into 2 pieces each.

Combine the olive oil, lemon zest and juice, garlic, mint, red pepper flakes, and black pepper in a large bowl. Toss in the calamari and stir well to coat. Refrigerate for 30 minutes, or until everything else is ready.

Put the chickpeas in a medium bowl, add the oil, vinegar, scallions, garlic, and mustard seeds, and stir to mix well. Season with salt and pepper and set aside.

93

For the olive pesto: Combine the oil, orange zest and juice, olive paste, jalapeños, and basil in a small bowl, mixing well. Set aside.

Using a sharp paring knife or serrated knife, cut off the top and bottom of each orange to expose the flesh. Stand each one upright on a work surface and slice off the skin and bitter white pith, working from top to bottom and following the natural curve of the fruit, then trim away any remaining pith. To remove the segments, carefully cut each one away from the membranes, sliding the knife down either side to release it. Put the orange segments in a bowl and set aside.

Preheat a gas grill or prepare a fire in a charcoal grill. Place a piastra (see page 9) on the grill to preheat. Wrap a clean brick in two layers of heavy-duty foil and set it on top of the piastra to heat for 10 minutes.

Meanwhile, pour the calamari into a colander and drain for 10 minutes.

Using pot holders or oven mitts, remove the brick from the piastra. Put a handful of the calamari pieces on the piastra, place the brick on top of them, and cook for 2 minutes, or until they are well charred. Lift off the brick and, using a spatula or tongs, carefully transfer the calamari to a clean bowl. Repeat with the remaining calamari in batches.

Cut the calamari bodies into rings if desired. Pour the olive pesto over the calamari and stir well. Put the chickpeas in a shallow serving bowl and top with the calamari. Sprinkle with the mint, scatter the orange segments over, and serve.

There's a lot going on in this dish: The calamari is tossed in a zesty marinade with lemon, black and red pepper, and fresh mint before it goes on the grill and then is finished with a spicy olive paste and served over a chickpea salad, with more fresh mint and orange sections for a citrusy contrast. The real secret here is the grilling method—the calamari is cooked on a piastra and under a brick, which means it really chars, and the char has all the flavor.

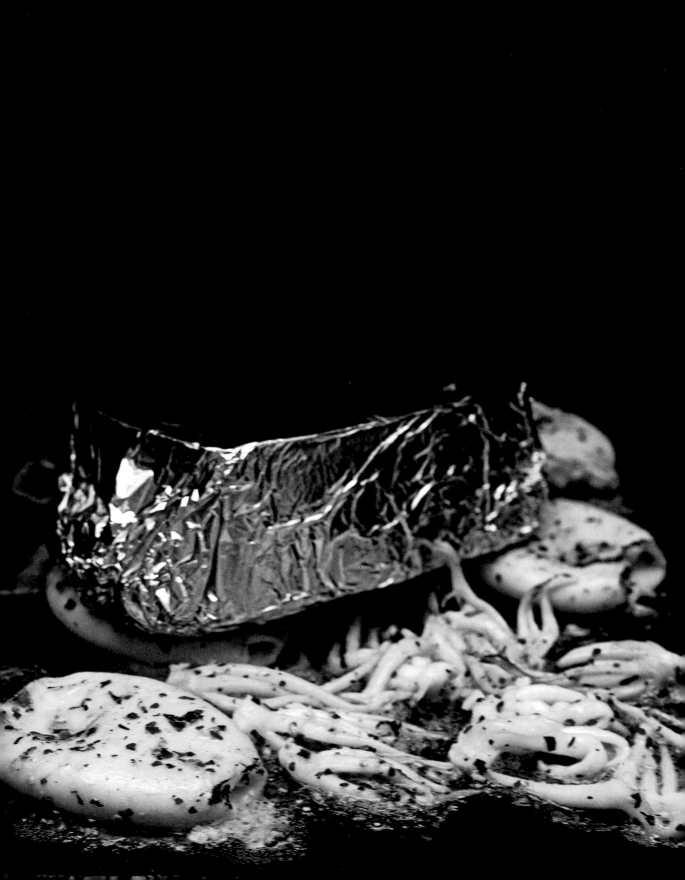

MUSSELS ALLA PIASTRA
WITH PROSCIUTTO BREAD CRUMBS

SERVES 6

4 pounds small mussels, such as Prince Edward Island (PEI), scrubbed and debearded

Grated zest and juice of 1 orange

Grated zest and juice of 1 lemon

1 jalapeño, thinly sliced

1 cup toasted bread crumbs

2 ounces thinly sliced prosciutto, coarsely chopped

1 bunch lemon thyme, leaves only

2 scallions, thinly sliced

2 tablespoons extra-virgin olive oil

PREHEAT A GAS GRILL or prepare a fire in a charcoal grill. Place a piastra (see page 9) on the grill to preheat for at least 15 minutes.

Put the mussels in a large metal bowl, add the orange and lemon zest and juice and the jalapeño, and toss gently. (If you don't have a metal bowl, toss in any large bowl, then use an upside-down roasting pan to cover the mussels when you cook them.) Set aside.

Place the bread crumbs, prosciutto, lemon thyme, and scallions in a food processor and zap until well mixed, six or seven pulses.

Pour the olive oil onto the piastra (if your piastra is not large enough, cook the mussels in two batches). Working quickly, dump the mussels (with everything else in the bowl) onto the piastra, scatter the bread crumb mixture over and around them, and cover with the inverted bowl. Remove the bowl after 2 minutes and gently stir the mussels around. Continue cooking, uncovered, for about 3 minutes longer, until they all open; transfer the mussels to a platter as they open (discard any that do not open). Scrape up any bread crumb mixture remaining on the piastra, scatter it over the mussels, and serve immediately.

The hotter the better for the piastra, so give it time to preheat—then the mussels will sizzle and jump and practically explode. (Even without the bread crumb mix, mussels cooked on the piastra are so good—toss them with the citrus and chili pepper before cooking, or just finish them with fresh lemon juice.) But if the grill and piastra are not superhot, the mussels will just steam in their own juices, and the result will not be nearly as good. Tossed with the mussels as they cook, the prosciutto bread crumbs become an interesting sticky mess that is simply delicious. Some of the crumbs will scorch and torch—and that's good.

CLAMS
IN CARTOCCIO

SERVES 6

¼ cup extra-virgin olive oil

4 ounces pancetta, cut into ⅛-inch dice (ask the butcher to slice the pancetta ⅛ inch thick when you buy it)

2 red bell peppers, cored, seeded, and cut into ¼-inch dice

6 garlic cloves, thinly sliced

2 to 3 teaspoons hot red pepper flakes

1 cup dry white wine

½ cup finely chopped fresh Italian parsley

3 pounds New Zealand cockles or small clams, such as Manilas, scrubbed

12 ripe Sungold or cherry tomatoes, halved

PREHEAT A GAS GRILL or prepare a fire in a charcoal grill.

In a 10- to 12-inch sauté pan, combine the oil and pancetta and cook over medium heat, stirring occasionally, until the pancetta is starting to brown, 4 to 5 minutes. Add the bell peppers, garlic, and pepper flakes and cook, stirring occasionally, just until the peppers are beginning to soften, about 3 minutes. Add the wine and bring to a boil. Stir in the parsley, remove from the heat, and set aside to cool completely.

Cut six 12-inch squares of heavy-duty foil. Lay out the squares on a large work surface and fold up the edges of each one to form a shallow bowl. Divide the clams among them, then divide the pancetta mixture, with its liquid, among them. Scatter 4 tomato halves over each pile. Bring the four corners of each foil packet up over the clams like a hobo sack and twist the top together securely, crimping the edges to create a tight seal.

Place the packs on the hottest part of the grill and wait until you can hear the juices bubbling, about 2 to 3 minutes, then let cook for 4 minutes longer. Transfer the packets to a large platter and serve, warning your guests of the piscatorial facial that awaits them.

Cooking shellfish *in cartoccio* is one of the easiest ways to prepare it, and one of the most fun, and it's virtually bulletproof as well. Even if they overcook slightly, their steamy environment will keep them moist—and if you have to hold them for a few minutes before serving, they will stay hot and won't dry out.

SHRIMP ROSEMARY
SPIEDINI ALLA ROMAGNOLA

SERVES 6

1 bunch Italian parsley, leaves only (about 2 cups loosely packed)

1 bunch basil, leaves only (about 2 cups packed)

2 cups fresh bread crumbs

½ teaspoon kosher salt

Freshly ground black pepper to taste

¼ cup plus 2 tablespoons extra-virgin olive oil

2 pounds large shrimp (21–30 per pound), peeled and deveined

12 large rosemary sprigs, prepared as skewers (see Note) and soaked in water for at least 2 hours, or overnight

2 lemons, cut into wedges

TOSS THE PARSLEY AND BASIL LEAVES into a food processor, add the bread crumbs, salt, pepper, and ¼ cup of the olive oil, and zap until the herbs are chopped and the bread crumbs look green. Transfer to a pie plate or wide shallow bowl, add the shrimp, and toss to coat well.

Skewer 4 or 5 shrimp on each rosemary sprig (the easiest way to do this is line up 4 or 5 shrimp at a time on a work surface and run a skewer through them; then separate them slightly so they will cook evenly). Dredge on both sides in the bread crumb mixture, place on a platter, and put in the refrigerator for 30 minutes.

Preheat a gas grill or prepare a fire in a charcoal grill. Put a piastra (see page 9) on the grill to preheat.

Spritz or brush the piastra with the remaining 2 tablespoons olive oil. Place the skewers on the piastra and cook, turning once, just until the shrimp are opaque throughout and some of the crumbs are browned, 2 to 3 minutes per side. Transfer to a serving platter and serve with the lemon wedges.

Note: It's easy to make skewers from rosemary sprigs. Choose large sturdy sprigs that are about 8 inches long. Pull off most of the leaves from each sprig, leaving a nice tuft of leaves at the top (use the remaining leaves in the dish you are making, or reserve for another use). Using a sharp knife, cut off the bottom of the sprig on a diagonal to give you a sharp point. The skewer will slide easily through the shrimp when you skewer them.

The rosemary skewers, which are easy to make, impart an herbal fragrance to the shrimp, and they look both rustic and elegant at the same time. *Alla romagnola* means that these spiedini are a specialty of Romagna, the eastern part of the region Emilia-Romagna.

WARM SHRIMP SALAD
WITH GREEN BEANS AND CHILIES

SERVES 6

2 pounds large shrimp (21–30 per pound), peeled and deveined

¼ cup plus 3 tablespoons extra-virgin olive oil

2 tablespoons black olive paste

1 teaspoon hot red pepper flakes

1 pound green beans or haricots verts, trimmed

1 cup (4 ounces) hazelnuts, coarsely chopped

1 red onion, halved lengthwise and very thinly sliced

2 red cayenne or other hot chili peppers, very thinly sliced

Grated zest and juice of 1 lemon

About 1 teaspoon freshly ground black pepper

PREHEAT A GAS GRILL or prepare a fire in a charcoal grill. Place a piastra (see page 9) on the grill to preheat.

Place the shrimp in a bowl, add 3 tablespoons of the olive oil, the olive paste, and red pepper flakes, and mix well with your hands to coat the shrimp. Set aside.

Bring a large pot of generously salted water to a boil. Set up an ice bath. Drop the beans into the boiling water and cook just until al dente, about 5 minutes. Drain and plunge into the ice bath to cool, then drain well.

Place the beans in a serving bowl, add the hazelnuts, red onion, and chilies, and toss to mix. Set aside.

Spread the shrimp on the piastra in a single layer (cook in two batches if necessary) and cook until pink and golden brown on the first side, about 2 minutes. Turn and cook until just cooked through, about 2 minutes longer.

Toss the shrimp into the bowl with the beans. Add the remaining ¼ cup olive oil and the lemon juice and zest and toss well. Season generously with black pepper, and serve warm or at room temperature.

One of my favorites. White beans are traditionally served with shrimp; the green beans are a fun variation. All the different flavors and textures really come together in this delicious salad. And the recipe doubles easily for a crowd, making it an excellent choice for a summer buffet.

GRILLED LOBSTER
WITH LEMON OIL

SERVES 6

LEMON OIL

1 cup extra-virgin olive oil

Grated zest and juice of 3 lemons

1 bunch marjoram

3 tablespoons limoncello or other lemon liqueur

Three 2-pound live spiny or Maine lobsters

Generous 4 cups trimmed arugula, washed and spun dry

Coarse sea salt

2 lemons, cut into wedges

COMBINE THE OLIVE OIL and lemon zest and juice in a small saucepan and bring just to a simmer over medium heat. Pour into a heat-proof bowl, add the marjoram and limoncello, and let cool.

As soon as the oil is cool, cover and refrigerate for at least 1 hour, or overnight.

Strain the oil and keep refrigerated until ready to use. It can be stored in the refrigerator in a tightly sealed jar for up to 10 days—no longer.

Preheat a gas grill or prepare a fire in a charcoal grill.

To kill the lobsters, hold each one firmly on a cutting board with the head toward you, plunge a sharp heavy knife into the center of the head, with the blade facing you, and quickly bring the knife down to the cutting board, splitting the front of the shell in half.

Place the lobsters shell side up on the hottest part of the grill and cook for 3 minutes. Turn over and cook for 3 minutes on the second side. Transfer to a cutting board.

Split the lobsters completely in half and remove the head sacs from each half. Being careful not to lose any of the tomalley—and roe, if the lobsters are female—gently anoint them on the flesh side with some of the fragrant lemon oil, using a pastry brush.

Place the lobsters shell side down on the grill and cook until nearly done, 6 to 7 minutes. Turn them flesh side down and cook for 1 minute longer, or until just cooked through.

Meanwhile, dress the arugula with ¼ cup of the lemon oil and a little coarse salt and pile in the center of a large serving platter.

Arrange the lobster over and around the arugula and garnish with the lemon wedges. Serve warm or at room temperature, with the remaining lemon oil on the side.

Simple but luxurious. Limoncello is a sweet Italian liqueur—buy a bottle to use for the lemon oil and keep the rest of it in the refrigerator or freezer to serve very cold as a *digestivo*.

SEA SCALLOPS
ALLA CAPRESE

SERVES 6

2 pounds mixed great heirloom tomatoes

24 fresh basil leaves

3 medium red onions, cut into 1-inch-thick slices

Kosher salt and freshly ground black pepper

5 to 6 tablespoons extra-virgin olive oil

12 giant diver scallops (about 2 ounces each)

Maldon salt or other coarse sea salt

1 lemon, cut in half

PREHEAT A GAS GRILL or prepare a fire in a charcoal grill. Place a piastra (see page 9) on the grill to preheat.

Slice the tomatoes creatively (leave very small ones whole, or halve them) and lay out on a platter. Tear the basil leaves over the tomatoes, strewing them about. Set aside.

Season the onion slices on both sides with salt and pepper. Place them on the hot dry piastra and cook, unmoved, for 7 to 10 minutes, until well charred on the first side. Using tongs, carefully turn the slices over and cook for 7 to 10 minutes on the second side, until well charred and softened. Transfer to a plate and let cool slightly, then separate the onion slices into smaller rings and scatter them over the tomatoes. Drizzle the whole mess with 3 to 4 tablespoons of the olive oil.

While the onions cook, carve a checkerboard pattern about ¼ inch deep into one side of each scallop. Season the scallops all over with salt and pepper, toss them in a bowl with the remaining 2 tablespoons oil, and stir gently to coat.

Place the scallops on the dry clean piastra, design side down, and cook for 5 to 7 minutes, unmoved, until almost cooked—they should be opaque almost all the way through. Flip them over and sear for just 30 seconds, then remove and arrange on the tomato salad.

Sprinkle the scallops and tomatoes with Maldon salt, squeeze the lemon halves over them, and serve.

Scoring the scallops before grilling makes them open up like a flower. The trick here is to cook the scallops 90 percent on the first side, until very well seared, then just give them a quick finish on the other side.

OCTOPUS
AND POTATO SALAD

SERVES 6

One 3-pound octopus (frozen octopus is fine), sac, beak, and eyes removed (you can have the fishmonger do this)

6 garlic cloves

2 dried Italian chilies or other hot chilies

1 pound medium Yellow Finn or Yukon Gold potatoes (4 or 5 potatoes)

½ cup plus 2 tablespoons extra-virgin olive oil

4 scallions, thinly sliced

1 medium red onion, thinly sliced

Grated zest and juice of 2 lemons

1 cup (8 ounces) pitted Gaeta olives

Kosher salt and freshly ground black pepper

PUT THE OCTOPUS, GARLIC, CHILIES, and 2 wine corks (the corks help tenderize the octopus) in a medium pot, add water to cover, and bring to a boil. Reduce the heat, cover, and simmer for 50 minutes to 1 hour, or until the thickest part of the octopus is tender when pierced with a knife. Drain and allow to cool.

Meanwhile, put the potatoes in a large saucepan of generously salted water and bring to a boil. Reduce the heat slightly and cook until the potatoes are just knife-tender, 12 to 15 minutes. Drain and let cool for about 5 minutes.

Peel and halve the warm potatoes and place in a medium bowl. Add ½ cup of the olive oil, the scallions, red onion, lemon zest and juice, and olives and stir gently to mix. Season with salt and pepper, and set aside.

Preheat a gas grill or prepare a fire in a charcoal grill.

Brush the octopus with the remaining 2 tablespoons oil and lay it over the hottest part of the grill. Cook for 9 to 12 minutes, unmoved, until nicely charred on the first side. Gently turn it over and cook for another 8 minutes, or until nicely charred on the second side.

Transfer the octopus to a cutting board and cut into 1½-inch pieces. Add to the potato salad and gently toss. Serve warm or at room temperature.

I love this dish. Surprise them the next time your friends ask you to bring the potato salad.

BABY OCTOPUS

WITH GIGANTE BEANS AND OLIVE-ORANGE VINAIGRETTE

SERVES 6

BEAN SALAD

Two 14-ounce cans gigante beans or butter beans, drained and rinsed, or 3½ cups cooked beans

3 garlic cloves, thinly sliced

2 scallions, thinly sliced

1 teaspoon fresh thyme leaves

¼ cup extra-virgin olive oil

Kosher salt and freshly ground black pepper

VINAIGRETTE

2 shallots, minced

¼ cup pitted Gaeta olives

¼ cup red wine vinegar

1 teaspoon hot red pepper flakes

Grated zest of 2 oranges

¼ cup extra-virgin olive oil

2 pounds baby octopus (26–40 per pound)

Extra-virgin olive oil

Kosher salt and freshly ground black pepper

1 small bunch chives, cut into 1-inch lengths

PREHEAT A GAS GRILL or prepare a fire in a charcoal grill.

Combine the beans, garlic, scallions, thyme, and olive oil in a medium bowl and mix well. Season with salt and pepper, and set aside. (The beans can be prepared up to a day ahead, covered, and refrigerated; bring to room temperature before serving.)

For the vinaigrette: Combine the shallots, olives, vinegar, red pepper flakes, and orange zest in a medium bowl and mix well. Gradually whisk in the olive oil. Set aside.

Toss the octopus with enough olive oil to coat lightly, and season well with salt and pepper. Arrange the octopi on the hottest part of the grill, leaving at least 1 inch between them, and grill, turning once, until crispy, about 4 minutes per side.

Mound the bean salad on a large platter. Arrange the octopus over and around the beans. Drizzle with half the vinaigrette and sprinkle with the chives. Serve with the remaining vinaigrette as a dipping sauce.

Baby octopus may be a little less intimidating than the big guy on page 108, perhaps a first step for your wussy friends. Goya now sells gigante beans labeled "habas grandes" or "butter beans," and they are excellent–do not be afraid of canned beans.

CHARRED TUNA SPIEDINI
WITH SPICY PEPPERS

MAKES 6 SPIEDINI

2 tablespoons fennel pollen or ground toasted fennel seeds

2 tablespoons dried oregano, crumbled

2 tablespoons sugar

1 tablespoon kosher salt

2 tablespoons freshly ground black pepper

2 pounds sushi-grade tuna, cut into 1-inch cubes

PEPPERS

3 tablespoons extra-virgin olive oil

1 medium red onion, thinly sliced

8 garlic cloves, smashed

3 red bell peppers, cored, seeded, and cut into ½-inch-wide strips

3 yellow bell peppers, cored, seeded, and cut into ½-inch-wide strips

4 jalapeños, thinly sliced

Kosher salt and freshly ground black pepper

3 tablespoons red wine vinegar

2 tablespoons fresh marjoram leaves

¼ cup extra-virgin olive oil

2 lemons, cut into wedges

IF USING BAMBOO SKEWERS, soak them in water for at least 30 minutes.

Mix the fennel pollen, oregano, sugar, salt, and pepper together in a large bowl. Toss in the tuna cubes and shake and toss in the mix to lightly coat, then dump them onto a platter. Thread 5 or 6 tuna cubes on each of 6 skewers, shaking off the excess herb rub and placing them about ½ inch apart so they will cook evenly. Put in the refrigerator for 30 minutes.

Preheat a gas grill or prepare a fire in a charcoal grill.

Meanwhile, for the peppers: In a 10- to 12-inch sauté pan, heat the olive oil over medium-high heat. Add the onion, garlic, bell peppers, jalapeños, and salt and pepper to taste and cook, stirring occasionally, until the onion and peppers are softened, about 7 to 9 minutes; reduce the heat slightly if the vegetables start to color. Add the vinegar and allow it to steam up, then immediately toss the peppers into a medium bowl and let cool for 10 minutes.

Add the marjoram leaves to the peppers and stir well. Season to taste with additional salt and/or pepper if necessary, and spoon the pepper stew onto a serving platter.

Lightly brush or drizzle the tuna cubes with the oil, turning the skewers as you do so. Place the skewers on the hottest part of the grill and cook for 1 minute, then carefully turn them over with tongs. Things may seem a little smoky and hectic—do not worry. Cook on the second side for 1 minute, and transfer to the platter with the peppers.

Garnish with the lemon wedges and serve immediately.

Fennel pollen, available from specialty spice purveyors (see Sources, page 232), is intensely aromatic, but if you lightly toast fennel seeds and grind them yourself, you will have a similar flavor. Make sure your grill is hot, hot, hot, and then cook the tuna for just a minute on each side, keeping it very rare and very succulent.

TUNA
LIKE FIORENTINA

SERVES 6

3 tuna steaks cut 2 to 2½ inches thick (about 3 pounds total)

2 tablespoons finely chopped fresh rosemary

2 tablespoons freshly ground black pepper

1 tablespoon plus 1 teaspoon kosher salt

1 teaspoon sugar

¼ cup extra-virgin olive oil

Great extra-virgin olive oil for drizzling

Coarse sea salt

REMOVE THE TUNA from the refrigerator to come to room temperature. Preheat a gas grill or prepare a fire in a charcoal grill.

In a small bowl, mix the rosemary, pepper, salt, and sugar well. Pour the olive oil onto a plate. Turn the tuna steaks in the oil to coat, then place on another plate and coat well on both sides with the herb rub, patting it so it adheres.

Place the steaks over the hottest part of the grill and cook, turning once, for 2 minutes per side for rare, 3 minutes per side for medium-rare. (If you want your tuna more cooked than that, throw the steaks directly into the trash bin and buy some cans of good tuna instead.) Remove the steaks to a platter and allow to rest for 5 minutes.

Cut the tuna into ¼-inch-thick slices and serve with great olive oil and coarse sea salt.

Poetic license—Florentines would never eat their tuna rare, they'd grill it until well-done or poach it slowly in olive oil. But, like *bistecca alla fiorentina*, this uses a big, thick cut and cooks it only until very rare. And the spice-crusted tuna, charred and striped with grill marks, does look a lot like a big steak. Allow the grilled tuna to rest, just like meat, so it's just above room temperature when you slice it. I like to serve this with Grilled Porcini (page 208) and Thousand-Ridges Japanese Eggplant (page 213).

MACKEREL "IN SCAPECE"

WITH AMALFI LEMON SALAD

SERVES 6

LEMON SALAD

2 thin-skinned lemons, scrubbed

2 tablespoons coarse sea salt

1 tablespoon sugar

1 tablespoon freshly ground black pepper

¼ cup extra-virgin olive oil

¼ cup fresh Italian parsley leaves cut into chiffonade (thin slivers)

2 pounds freshest-possible king mackerel fillet, skin on

½ cup extra-virgin olive oil

Kosher salt and freshly ground black pepper

1 cup red wine vinegar

1 medium red onion, cut into ⅛-inch-thick rounds

½ cup sugar

2 tablespoons fresh lemon thyme leaves

1 tablespoon hot red pepper flakes

USING A VERY SHARP KNIFE, cut the lemons into paper-thin slices. (The salad looks prettiest with whole slices, but you may find it easier to cut the lemons lengthwise in half first and then into paper-thin half slices.)

Layer the lemon slices in a large shallow baking dish. Sprinkle evenly first with the salt, then with the sugar, and then the pepper. Allow to sit for 10 minutes.

Pour the olive oil evenly over the lemons. Allow to sit for 1 hour at room temperature.

Preheat a gas grill or prepare a fire in a charcoal grill.

Cut the mackerel into approximately 2-inch pieces. Put them on a small baking sheet, brush on all sides with 2 tablespoons of the olive oil, and season with salt and pepper.

Place the mackerel pieces skin side down on the hottest part of the grill, leaving space between them, and cook, unmoved, until the cooked look has crept up the sides but the very top is still translucent, 3 to 5 minutes for thinner pieces, 5 to 7 minutes for thicker pieces. As the pieces cook, carefully remove them with tongs or a spatula and place raw side down in one layer in a shallow serving dish.

Combine the vinegar, the remaining ¼ cup plus 2 tablespoons olive oil, the red onion slices, sugar, thyme, and red pepper flakes in a medium saucepan and bring to a boil. Cook for 1 minute, then remove from the heat.

Pour the hot vinegar mixture over the mackerel fillets and allow to stand for 3 to 5 minutes, just until the raw bottom part has cooked through.

Add the parsley to the lemons, toss to mix well, and place on a serving platter. Stack the mackerel pieces on top of the lemon salad. Drizzle some of the vinegar mixture over the fish, and serve warm or at room temperature.

Scapece was originally a method of preserving fish for a week or two, and it still can be, but I love it for its vibrant acid rush; it really tunes me up. Try to find organic lemons, but regular lemons will be OK if you scrub them well. The longer the lemon salad sits, the sweeter it will be. If you can't get high-quality mackerel, you can substitute bluefish or even fresh sardines. As with any oily fish, freshness is key: day 1, the fish is great; day 2, it won't be.

MONKFISH IN PROSCIUTTO
WITH PESTO FREGOLA

SERVES 6

2 pieces monkfish tail (bone and skin removed, and all of the nasty stuff too; about 2½ pounds total)

Kosher salt and freshly ground black pepper

8 ounces thinly sliced prosciutto

1 pound fregola (see page 17), acini di pepe, or orzo

1 cup Pesto (page 50)

2 red bell peppers, cored, seeded, and cut into ¼-inch dice

¼ cup extra-virgin olive oil

¼ cup pine nuts, toasted until golden brown

RINSE THE MONKFISH AND PAT DRY. Season with salt and pepper.

Arrange half of the prosciutto slices on a work surface, overlapping them to make a rectangle large enough to enclose one of the monkfish tails (use enough prosciutto to enclose the monkfish securely; you may have a couple of slices left over). Lay the fish in the center and fold the prosciutto up and around it to make a tight roulade. If necessary, secure with butcher's twine or toothpicks. Repeat with the second tail. Set seam side down on a plate and refrigerate for 1 hour.

Preheat a gas grill or prepare a fire in a charcoal grill. Place a piastra (see page 9) on the grill to preheat.

Meanwhile, in a large pot, bring 6 quarts of water to a boil and add 2 tablespoons salt. Set up an ice water bath. Drop the fregola into the boiling water and cook until just al dente. Drain and immediately refresh in the ice bath; when it is cool, drain the fregola extremely well.

In a large bowl, toss the fregola with the pesto and red peppers. Set aside.

Brush each prosciutto-wrapped tail with 1 tablespoon of the olive oil. Place on the piastra and cook for 6 minutes, unmoved. Gently roll each one over 90 degrees and cook for 4 minutes. Repeat twice, for a total cooking time of about 18 minutes; the internal temperature should be about 150°F in the thickest part of the fish. Transfer to a platter and allow to rest for 10 minutes.

Cut the tails into ¾-inch slices and arrange nicely on top of the fregola. Drizzle with the remaining 2 tablespoons olive oil, sprinkle with the pine nuts, and serve.

So delicious, with crisp, salty, porky prosciutto enveloping the mild, tender fish. Refrigerating the fish before cooking it helps make its "shirt" of prosciutto to adhere. Nutty, flavorful fregola tossed with pesto adds another dimension.

SWORDFISH
INVOLTINI
SICILIAN-STYLE

SERVES 6

TOMATO SALAD

- 1 pound ripe tomatoes, cut into ¼-inch cubes
- ½ cup Gaeta olives (you can pit them, but I don't)
- ¼ cup salt-packed capers, rinsed and drained
- ¼ cup currants
- 2 tablespoons pine nuts, toasted until golden brown
- 1½ teaspoons hot red pepper flakes
- ¼ cup extra-virgin olive oil

  Kosher salt

- 2 oranges
- 1 cup fresh bread crumbs
- ¼ cup finely chopped fresh Italian parsley
- ¼ cup extra-virgin olive oil

  Kosher salt and freshly ground black pepper

  One 2-pound skinless swordfish steak,
  cut horizontally into 6 thin slices
  (about ⅓ inch thick; see the note on page 125)

TOASTING PINE NUTS

Toasting pine nuts brings out their flavor. To toast them, put them on a small baking sheet or in a pie pan and toast in a preheated 350°F oven for 5 to 7 minutes, stirring occasionally, until golden brown. Once the nuts start to color, they will darken rapidly, so keep an eye on them, and transfer them a plate to cool as soon as they are done. If you need only a couple of tablespoons of toasted nuts, you can toast them in a small heavy skillet over medium-low heat, stirring frequently, for about 5 minutes, or until golden brown. Pour onto a plate and let cool.

IN A MEDIUM BOWL, combine the tomatoes, olives, capers, currants, pine nuts, pepper flakes, and olive oil and stir gently to mix. Set aside (don't refrigerate).

Grate the zest from the oranges; set aside. Using a sharp paring knife or serrated knife, cut off the top and bottom of 1 orange to expose the flesh (reserve the other orange for another use). Stand it upright on a work surface and slice off the skin and bitter white pith, working from top to bottom and following the natural curve of the fruit, then trim away any remaining pith. To remove the segments, carefully cut each one away from the membranes, sliding the knife down either side to release it. Set aside in a small bowl.

In a small bowl, combine the bread crumbs, parsley, reserved orange zest, 2 tablespoons of the olive oil, ½ teaspoon salt, and pepper to taste, mixing well with your hands or a fork.

Cut twelve 9-inch-long pieces of kitchen twine. Season each slice of swordfish with salt and pepper. Lay out on a work surface and divide the bread crumb mixture among the slices, spreading it evenly. Starting from a narrow end, carefully roll each one up like a jelly roll and tie with 2 pieces of twine. Place on a plate and refrigerate for 20 to 30 minutes.

Preheat a gas grill or prepare a fire in a charcoal grill.

Brush the swordfish rolls all over with the remaining 2 tablespoons olive oil and season again with salt and pepper. Place on the hottest part of the grill and cook for 2 minutes. Gently turn over 90 degrees with tongs and cook for 1 minute, then repeat twice to cook on all sides.

To serve, season the tomato salad with a little salt and spread out on a platter. Place the involtini on the tomatoes, and garnish with the orange segments.

Sicilians make involtini out of almost everything. This is a summery version of a traditional swordfish involtini, with the stuffed rollatini cooked on the grill and accompanied by a fresh tomato salad packed with typical Sicilian flavors: olives, capers, currants, and pine nuts.

SWORDFISH

PAILLARDS WITH ARUGULA AND TOMATOES

SERVES 6

One 1½-pound skinless swordfish steak, cut horizontally into 6 thin slices (about ¼ inch thick; see note below)

3½ tablespoons extra-virgin olive oil

Kosher salt and freshly ground black pepper

3 cups trimmed arugula, washed and spun dry

1 pound super-ripe cherry or grape tomatoes, halved

2 teaspoons black or brown mustard seeds (available in Indian markets, or see Sources, page 232)

Scant 1 tablespoon red wine vinegar

PREHEAT A GAS GRILL or prepare a fire in a charcoal grill.

Brush the swordfish on both sides with 2 tablespoons of the olive oil and season with salt and pepper. Place the swordfish paillards on the grill and cook for 1 minute, unmoved, then gently flip and cook for 15 seconds on the second side, or until just cooked through (watch carefully, the cooking goes very quickly). Transfer to a large platter.

In a medium bowl, gently toss the arugula with the cherry tomatoes and mustard seeds, then add the remaining 1½ tablespoons olive oil and the vinegar and gently toss to mix well. Season with salt and pepper.

Arrange the salad on top of the swordfish and serve immediately.

Simple, delicate, and colorful, this is one of those dishes defined by the quality of the ingredients. Be sure the tomatoes are really ripe and the swordfish is really fresh. You can also make the vinaigrette with fresh lemon juice instead of red wine vinegar. Any good fishmonger will be happy to cut the fish into paillards (thin slices), but if you have to slice it yourself, put it in the freezer first for about 15 minutes to firm it slightly and make cutting it easier.

GRILLED WHOLE BRANZINO
WITH SALSA VERDE

SERVES 6

Three 2-pound branzino, cleaned and scaled

1 large fennel bulb

2 tablespoons fresh thyme leaves

2 tablespoons fresh oregano leaves

1 cup (8 ounces) pitted Gaeta olives

Kosher salt and freshly ground black pepper

SALSA VERDE

2 cups fresh Italian parsley leaves

½ cup fresh basil leaves

1 garlic clove

¼ cup fresh bread crumbs

¼ cup capers, drained

1 salt-packed anchovy, filleted, rinsed, and drained, or 2 oil-packed anchovy fillets, drained

3 tablespoons white wine vinegar

1 cup extra-virgin olive oil

Kosher salt

2 to 3 tablespoons extra-virgin olive oil

RINSE THE FISH AND PAT DRY. Use kitchen shears to remove the top and bottom fins. Set aside.

Trim the fennel bulb, halve lengthwise, and cut out most of the core (reserve a few fronds to add to the stuffing if you like). Using a mandoline or other vegetable slicer, shave the fennel into thin slices. Transfer to a large bowl, add the thyme, oregano, olives, and salt and pepper to taste, and mix well.

Stuff each fish generously with one-third of the fennel mixture. The stuffing will almost be spilling out; secure the cavities with a toothpick or two if necessary. Place the fish in a shallow casserole or baking dish, cover, and refrigerate.

Put the parsley, basil, garlic, bread crumbs, capers, anchovies, and vinegar in a food processor and zap until the herbs are coarsely chopped. With the motor running, drizzle in the olive oil until a smooth sauce forms. Season with salt if it needs it, and set aside. (The sauce can be stored just like pesto, in a tightly sealed jar topped with a thin layer of extra-virgin olive oil, for several weeks in the refrigerator.)

Preheat a gas grill or prepare a fire in a charcoal grill.

Oil the grill grate, using a clean rag dipped in oil or a basting brush. Brush the fish with the olive oil and place them gently on the hottest part of the grill. Cook, unmoved, for 4 minutes, then carefully lift them with tongs, turn 90 degrees, so you will get nice grill marks, and cook for 4 minutes. Gently turn the fish over and repeat the same procedure on the second side, cooking until the flesh is opaque throughout (check the flesh nearest the bone to make sure). Transfer to a platter and allow to rest for 5 minutes.

Show off the whole fish at the table, then fillet the fish and put one fillet and some stuffing on each plate. Serve with the salsa verde.

Italians rarely serve any sauce at all—other than good olive oil, maybe a squeeze of lemon—with fish, but a beautiful grilled whole branzino can more than stand up to *salsa verde*, the classic green herb sauce. The salsa takes it to a whole other level, but be sure to try the branzino both with and without, so that you really understand your fish.

SALMON
IN CARTOCCIO
WITH ASPARAGUS, CITRUS, AND THYME

SERVES 6

2 oranges

2 lemons

½ cup extra-virgin olive oil

2 salt-packed anchovies, filleted, rinsed, and drained,
or 4 oil-packed anchovy fillets, drained

4 garlic cloves, thinly sliced

6 spears jumbo asparagus, tough bottoms snapped off, stalks cut
on the diagonal into ¼-inch-thick slices, tips halved lengthwise

Kosher salt and freshly ground black pepper

Six 4- to 5-ounce wild salmon fillets

1 tablespoon fresh thyme leaves

¾ cup dry white wine

USING A SHARP PARING KNIFE OR SERRATED KNIFE, cut off the
top and bottom of each orange and lemon to expose the flesh.
Stand each one upright on a work surface and slice off the skin
and bitter white pith, working from top to bottom and following the natural curve of the fruit, then trim away any remaining
pith. To remove the segments, carefully cut each one away from
the membranes, sliding the knife down either side to release it.
Set aside.

In a medium sauté pan, heat 2 tablespoons of the olive oil over
medium-low heat. Add the anchovies and garlic and cook, stirring, until the anchovies are falling apart and the garlic is lightly

browned, 2 to 3 minutes. Add the asparagus and cook, stirring, just until the slices are barely tender in the center, about 1 minute. Season with salt if necessary and pepper, remove from the heat, and let cool.

Cut six 12-inch squares of heavy-duty aluminum foil. Fold each one in half to mark the center, then unfold it. Season the fish fillets aggressively on both sides with salt and pepper. Drizzle 1 tablespoon of the remaining olive oil over the bottom half of each piece of foil and top with one-sixth of the asparagus mixture. Place the fish on top and arrange about 3 orange sections and 2 lemon sections (or half-sections) on top of each fillet. Sprinkle with the thyme.

Fold up ½ inch or so of the three bottom edges of each packet to make a shallow container, and drizzle 2 tablespoons of the white wine over and around each fillet. Fold over the top of the foil to cover the salmon, fold over about ¼ inch of the open edges together to seal them, and then make a double fold for a tight seal.

Place the packets on the hottest part of the grill and wait until you can hear the wine bubbling, about 2 to 3 minutes, then cook for 5 minutes more. Transfer the packets to a large platter or a baking sheet and allow them to stand for 5 minutes.

Place a *cartoccio* on each plate and serve, letting your guests cut open the fragrant packets themselves.

This is a lovely dish, simple to make but far more than the sum of its parts. Cooked *in cartoccio* (traditionally wrapped in parchment paper, here in aluminum foil for the grill), the salmon fillets grill-poach in their own little steam baths and emerge succulent and flavorful. Listening is always part of cooking, and for this recipe you really need to rely on the audio—when you hear the wine bubbling, you know you're in the right spot.

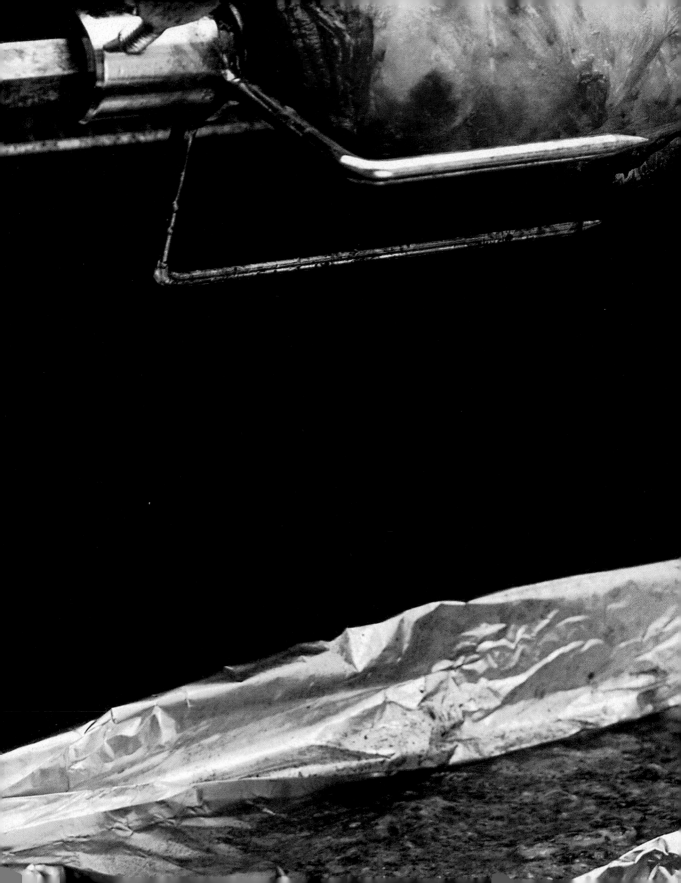

POULTRY

Everyone loves grilled chicken, although Italians are more likely to grill smaller birds such as game hens and quail. But we, unlike most Italians, are lucky enough to have a ready and ever-increasing supply of farm-raised organic and free-range chickens and other birds that have succulent, tasty meat and take perfectly to grilling. Forget that image of "barbecued" chicken charred black on the outside and still raw inside—the recipes in this chapter will give you juicy, tender results.

Most of these recipes call for marinating the bird, whole or cut-up, before grilling: the Chicken alla Diavola in a zippy mix of hot red pepper flakes, sweet Spanish smoked paprika, and citrus zest and juice; the Spicy Black-Pepper-Coated Drumsticks in a buttermilk marinade seasoned with Tabasco sauce, fennel seeds, and black pepper. For Il Galletto al Mattone, marinated butterflied whole chickens are grilled under the weight of a brick, a classic technique that results in incredibly crisp skin and moist flesh. The Guinea Hen Breasts with Rosemary and Pesto are fragrant with some of my favorite flavors, and the Quail (with Artichokes Vinaigrette) are marinated in a delicate combination of balsamic vinegar, olive oil, honey, and thyme that makes it easy to cook the little birds perfectly.

If you have never tried rotisserie cooking, the results you will get by spit-roasting whole birds are reason enough to try it (rotisserie attachments that fit most grills are readily available and relatively inexpensive; see page 9 for more on this). As the chicken or other bird rotates on the spit over the hot grill, it "self-bastes," and you end up with amazingly succulent meat—there's a reason you see chickens rotating on a spit in every butcher shop in small towns across the entire rural landscape in Italy. And when I was growing up in Seattle, we knew that Sunday supper was always going to be special if we could hear the sound of the whirring spinner with a couple of chickens on it through the late-afternoon calm. They were always simply perfection, and the delicious Spit-Roasted Chicken with Wine Grapes and Panzanella just may become your go-to recipe for any and every occasion. Once you've tried the Duck with Orange and Rosemary, you may find yourself cooking duck often. And spit-roasting Turkey Breast Porchetta-Style gives this too often boring meat a whole new personality.

IL GALLETTO
AL MATTONE
(CHICKEN COOKED UNDER A BRICK)

SERVES 6

2 young chickens (about 3 pounds each)

3 tablespoons fennel pollen or ground toasted fennel seeds

¼ cup coarse sea salt or kosher salt

1 tablespoon freshly ground black pepper

1 tablespoon chopped fresh thyme

¼ cup extra-virgin olive oil

About ½ cup chopped fresh Italian parsley

Lemon wedges for serving

USING KITCHEN SHEARS OR A SHARP KNIFE, cut down along both sides of the backbone of each chicken and remove it. Turn the chickens skin side up and press down hard on them with your palms to crack the breastbones and flatten them. Remove the excess fat and pat the chickens dry with paper towels.

In a small bowl, mix together the fennel pollen, salt, pepper, and thyme. Pat the mixture onto both sides of the chickens, coating them generously. Wrap each one tightly in plastic wrap, place on a baking sheet or in a baking dish, and refrigerate for 12 hours.

An hour before you are ready to grill, remove the chicken from the refrigerator.

Prepare a gas or charcoal grill for indirect grilling. Wrap two clean bricks in a double thickness of heavy-duty aluminum foil and place them on the hot part of the grill to preheat.

Gently blot the chickens dry. Rub the birds all over with the olive oil.

Using pot holders or oven mitts, move the bricks to the side of the grill. Oil the grill rack, using a clean rag dipped in oil or a basting brush. Place the chickens skin side down on the line midway between coals and no coals. Place a brick on top of each chicken, cover the grill, and cook for 10 minutes. Move the bricks to the side of the grill again, carefully lift up each chicken, making sure that the skin doesn't tear (gently slide a thin spatula under the chicken to detach it if necessary), and place skin side up on the hot part of the grill. Place the bricks on top again, cover the grill, and cook for 15 minutes, being careful to snuff any flare-ups with a squirt gun (or, as in my case, a beer).

Remove the bricks, carefully turn the chickens over, and cook, still on the hot part of the grill, for 5 minutes more, or until the thickest part of the thigh registers 165°F. Transfer the chickens to a platter and let rest for 5 to 10 minutes.

Sprinkle the chicken with the parsley and serve with lemon wedges.

Butterflying a whole chicken and weighting it with a brick as it cooks, whether in a skillet or on the grill, is a classic technique in Italy. The pressure of the brick when the skin is toward the flame makes the skin incredibly crisp, and the split chicken cooks quickly, so the meat remains succulent and juicy.

CHICKEN
ALLA DIAVOLA

SERVES 6

Grated zest and juice of 4 lemons

Grated zest and juice of 2 oranges

½ cup extra-virgin olive oil

5 tablespoons hot red pepper flakes

2 tablespoons sweet pimentón (Spanish smoked paprika)

2 young chickens (about 3 pounds each), cut into 8 pieces each, excess fat removed

Kosher salt and freshly ground black pepper

1 to 2 tablespoons hot pimentón (Spanish smoked paprika)

IN A SMALL BOWL, combine the lemon and orange zest and juice, olive oil, red pepper flakes, and sweet pimentón and stir to mix well. Place the chicken pieces in a baking dish large enough to hold them comfortably and pour the marinade over them, turning to coat. Cover and marinate in the refrigerator for at least 1 hour, or up to 6 hours, turning the pieces occasionally.

Preheat a gas grill or prepare a fire in a charcoal grill.

Remove the chicken from the marinade, draining it well, and pat dry with paper towels (to prevent flare-ups on the grill). Season the pieces generously with salt and with pepper to taste.

Place the chicken skin side down on the grill, cover the grill, and cook, turning occasionally and moving the pieces as necessary for even cooking, for 25 to 30 minutes, or until the skin is dark golden brown and the juices run clear when pierced at the thickest part. As the different pieces cook through (the wings and thighs will probably take the least time), move them to a cooler part of the grill to keep warm.

Transfer the chicken to a platter, sprinkling the pieces generously with hot pimentón. Serve hot or at room temperature.

Real *diavola* is very spicy, but if you want to tune it down a little, that's OK too.

CHICKEN THIGHS
WITH SNAP PEAS AND AGLIATA

SERVES 6

12 garlic cloves, crushed

½ cup plus 3 tablespoons extra-virgin olive oil

2 salt-packed anchovies, filleted, rinsed, and patted dry, or 4 oil-packed anchovy fillets, drained

½ cup chopped fresh Italian parsley

2 cups fresh bread crumbs

12 boneless, skinless chicken thighs

3 shallots, sliced ¼ inch thick

½ teaspoon anchovy paste

1 pound snap peas, blanched in boiling water just until bright green, chilled in an ice bath, and drained

Olio Piccante (page 33) for drizzling

COMBINE THE GARLIC, ½ cup of the oil, the anchovies, parsley, and bread crumbs in a food processor and zap until smoothish.

Put the chicken thighs in a large bowl and sprinkle with the bread crumb mixture, turning to coat well. Arrange in a single layer on a platter and put in the refrigerator for 15 minutes.

Prepare a gas or charcoal grill for indirect grilling.

Place the chicken thighs skinned side up on the cooler part of the grill, cover the grill, and grill, turning once, until the chicken is cooked through, about 15 minutes per side.

Meanwhile, heat the remaining 3 tablespoons oil in a 10- to 12-inch sauté pan over medium heat. Add the shallots and anchovy paste and cook, stirring occasionally, until the shallots are soft, about 5 minutes. Add the snap peas and cook, stirring, just until heated through. Transfer the snap peas to a platter and set aside.

Arrange the thighs on top of the snap peas and serve with a drizzle of olio piccante.

These chicken thighs are coated with a garlicky bread crumb mixture and cooked slowly over the cooler part of the grill so you end up with juicy meat and toasted herbed crust. (Be sure to scoop up all the delightful little clumps of flavorful crumbs from the grill and scatter them over the chicken.) Start the thighs boned side down so that by the time you flip them over, the "presentation side" will have dried a bit and won't stick to the grill.

DRUMSTICKS

SERVES 6

12 chicken drumsticks

Kosher salt

½ cup buttermilk

2 tablespoons Tabasco sauce, preferably chipotle

1 tablespoon fennel seeds, lightly crushed in a spice or coffee grinder

2 tablespoons freshly ground black pepper

2 fennel bulbs

4 ounces Gorgonzola dolce

¼ cup red wine vinegar

½ cup extra-virgin olive oil

PREHEAT THE OVEN TO 400°F.

Place the drumsticks on a baking sheet and season all over with salt. Bake for 20 minutes (25 minutes for very large drumsticks).

In a medium bowl, stir together the buttermilk, Tabasco, fennel seeds, and pepper. Set a wire rack over a small baking sheet.

As soon as the drumsticks come out of the oven, toss them, in batches, into the buttermilk and turn to coat, then place skin side up on the rack to drain. Spoon a little of the mixture, with fennel seeds and pepper, over each one, and set aside. (The drumsticks can be baked and marinated up to a day ahead; leave them on the rack, cover, and refrigerate. Bring to room temperature before grilling.)

Preheat a gas grill or prepare a fire in a charcoal grill.

Trim the fennel bulbs, cut lengthwise in half, and cut out the core. Cut into ¼-inch-wide bâtonnets and toss into a bowl of ice water.

Crumble the Gorgonzola into a small bowl and mash with a fork. Add the vinegar and stir until fairly smooth. Drizzle in the oil, stirring. Pour into shallow bowls for dipping.

Place the drumsticks on the hottest part of the grill, cover the grill, and cook, turning occasionally at first and then more often as they start to caramelize, until cooked through, 10 to 12 minutes.

Put the drumsticks on a platter. Drain the fennel sticks, pat dry, and place next to the wings. Serve with the Gorgonzola dressing.

Buffalo wings go to Italy: drumsticks in a spicy buttermilk marinade, red wine–Gorgonzola dressing, and fennel sticks standing in for the celery.

QUAIL
WITH ARTICHOKES VINAIGRETTE

SERVES 6

1½ cups extra-virgin olive oil

½ cup plus 2 tablespoons balsamic vinegar

2 tablespoons honey

1 tablespoon dried thyme, crumbled

2 tablespoons freshly ground black pepper, plus more to taste

12 semiboneless quail

1 medium red onion, finely chopped

6 garlic cloves, smashed

24 fresh mint leaves

1 cup dry white wine

Grated zest and juice of 2 lemons

12 baby artichokes

Kosher salt

IN A LARGE BAKING DISH, combine 1 cup of the olive oil, ½ cup of the vinegar, the honey, thyme, and pepper. Add the quail and turn to coat. Refrigerate for at least 4 hours, or overnight, turning occasionally.

Combine the onion, garlic, 12 of the mint leaves, the wine, ¼ cup of the olive oil, and the lemon zest and juice in a large saucepan. Trim the artichokes: pull off the tough outer leaves from each one, then cut off the top ½ inch of the remaining leaves. Trim the stem with a paring knife, cutting off the tough outer layer, then trim the base of the artichoke, removing any dark green parts. Cut the artichoke into quarters and drop into the saucepan; stir to coat as you add the remaining trimmed artichokes.

Add enough water to cover the artichokes, put a pan lid on top of the artichokes to keep them submerged, and bring to a boil. Cover, reduce the heat, and simmer for 5 minutes, or until the artichokes are just tender. Let cool in the cooking liquid.

Drain the artichokes and transfer to a bowl. Add the remaining 12 mint leaves, ¼ cup oil, and 2 tablespoons vinegar and season with salt and pepper. Transfer to a platter and set aside.

Preheat a gas grill or prepare a fire in a charcoal grill.

Drain the quail and pat dry. Season with salt and pepper. Place breast side down on the hottest part of the grill, cover the grill, and cook, unmoved, for 4 to 5 minutes, until golden brown. Turn the quail over and cook for 2 minutes, or until cooked to medium. Arrange the quail on the artichokes and serve immediately.

Rare quail tastes odd, well-done tastes dusty—medium is perfect.

GUINEA HEN BREASTS
WITH ROSEMARY AND PESTO

SERVES 6

½ cup plus 2 tablespoons extra-virgin olive oil

6 garlic cloves, thinly sliced

¼ cup chopped fresh rosemary

½ cup Pesto (page 50)

1 tablespoon hot red pepper flakes

6 single boneless guinea hen breasts with skin (or substitute skin-on boneless chicken breasts)

Kosher salt and freshly ground black pepper

IN A SMALL BOWL, combine ½ cup of the olive oil, the garlic, rosemary, pesto, and red pepper flakes and mix well.

Carefully slip your fingers under the skin of each guinea hen breast to loosen it without tearing or completely detaching it. Put the breasts in a large bowl, pour the marinade over them, and carefully rub it all over the breasts and under the skin, then smooth the skin back over the breasts. Cover and refrigerate for at least 4 hours; overnight is best.

When ready to cook, remove the guinea hen breasts from the marinade, brushing off the excess, place on a plate, and allow to sit at room temperature for 30 minutes.

Preheat a gas grill or prepare a fire in a charcoal grill.

Brush the breasts with the remaining 2 tablespoons oil and season aggressively all over with salt and pepper. Place skin side down on the hottest part of the grill, cover, and cook, unmoved, for 2 to 3 minutes. Gently lift each breast, rotate it 90 degrees to form beautiful grill marks, and cook for 2 to 3 minutes more, until well marked and golden brown. Gently flip over and grill until cooked through but still very juicy, 3 to 5 minutes more; the internal temperature of the thickest part of the breasts should be 160°F (160° to 165°F for chicken). Transfer to a platter and serve.

Guinea hens are smaller than most American chickens, and they have more flavor. You will never see me cook boneless chicken breasts, but I do grill boneless guinea hen breasts (if you can't get guinea hen, though, you can make the dish with chicken). The only tricky part is making sure not to overdo it, since once you've taken the bones out, it's easy to overcook the meat. Just pay attention, and pull them off the fire when they are deep brown but still very juicy.

TURKEY SAUSAGES

WITH SAGE FLATBREADS AND MOSTARDA

SERVES 10

DOUGH

3¼ cups all-purpose flour, plus extra for dusting

2 teaspoons instant or rapid-rise yeast

1 tablespoon salt

1 tablespoon sugar

2½ tablespoons finely minced fresh sage

1 cup warm water

¼ cup dry white wine, at room temperature

2 tablespoons plus 1 teaspoon extra-virgin olive oil

10 turkey sausages (not precooked; I like fennel seeds in them)

Mostarda di Cremona (see page 18) for serving

Hot purple horseradish for serving

IN A LARGE BOWL, combine the flour, yeast, salt, sugar, and sage and mix well. Make a well in the center of the dry ingredients and add the warm water, wine, and olive oil. Using a wooden spoon, stir the wet ingredients into the dry until the mixture is too stiff to stir, then mix with your hands in the bowl until the dough comes together and pulls away from the sides of the bowl.

Lightly dust a work surface with flour and turn the dough out. Knead gently, dusting the work surface lightly with more flour as necessary, for 5 minutes, or until the dough is smooth, elastic, and only slightly sticky.

149

Oil a large clean bowl, add the dough, and turn to coat with oil. Cover the bowl with plastic wrap or a kitchen towel, set in a warm part of the kitchen, and let the dough rise until doubled in size, about 1 hour.

Gently punch down the dough, turn out onto a cutting board or work surface, and cut into 10 pieces. Roll each piece under your palm into a ball, and place on a lightly oiled baking sheet. Cover loosely with oiled plastic wrap and let rise in a warm spot for 30 minutes (the dough will not double in size).

Preheat a gas grill or prepare a fire in a charcoal grill.

On a lightly floured surface, using a floured rolling pin or your hands, roll or press each ball of dough into a 6-inch round (if a piece of dough resists or shrinks back, let it rest briefly while you roll out another piece, then return to the first one). Place the rounds on the hottest part of the grill (in batches if necessary) and cook for 1 to 1½ minutes, or until puffy and golden brown on the first side. Turn over and cook until the second side is spotted with brown, 1 to 1½ minutes. Transfer to a large platter or a baking sheet and let rest while you cook the sausages.

Prick each sausage five or six times and place on the cooler part of the grill. Grill, rolling the sausages around to cook on all sides, until cooked through, 12 to 15 minutes. Transfer to a platter.

Toss the flatbreads onto the grill for a minute or so to warm them up, then transfer to the platter or pile in a basket. Serve with the mostarda and horseradish.

These little sage flatbreads are very easy and will work with just about anything from the grill. Make sandwiches with turkey or other sausages, grilled meats, whatever you like. Look for good turkey sausages at a butcher's or specialty market; be sure the ones you buy are not the precooked type.

SPIT-ROASTED
CHICKEN
WITH WINE GRAPES AND PANZANELLA

SERVES 4

One 3½- to 4-pound chicken

½ lemon

RUB

1 tablespoon sweet pimentón (Spanish smoked paprika)

2 teaspoons rubbed sage

1 teaspoon ground cumin

2 teaspoons coarse sea salt

2 teaspoons freshly ground black pepper

2 tablespoons extra-virgin olive oil

PANZANELLA

12 ounces day-old Italian peasant bread, with crust, cut into ¾-inch cubes (about 8 cups)

2 large tomatoes (about 1 pound), cut into ½-inch dice

2 kirby cucumbers, thinly sliced

1 medium red onion, cut lengthwise in half and then into ⅛-inch-thick slices

½ cup extra-virgin olive oil

¼ cup red wine vinegar

Kosher salt and freshly ground black pepper

10 fresh basil leaves, torn

3 bunches wine grapes, such as Sangiovese

PREPARE A GAS OR CHARCOAL GRILL for rotisserie cooking over indirect medium heat (or according to the instructions for your grill). Set up the drip pan under the center of the spit.

Remove the excess fat from the chicken and pat the chicken dry with paper towels. Rub the skin with the lemon half; reserve the lemon half. Mix all the rub ingredients together in a small bowl, and rub 2 teaspoons of the mixture inside the cavity of the chicken. Place what is left of the lemon half inside the cavity and truss the chicken. Brush the skin all over with the olive oil, then massage the remaining rub mixture into the bird.

Place the chicken on the spit and secure it with the clamps (if possible, run the clamps through the thighs of the chicken—the clamps will conduct heat so the thighs will cook more quickly and there will be less chance of the breast overcooking). Attach the spit to the rotisserie mechanism, cover the grill, and cook the chicken until the skin is a deep golden brown and the thickest part of the thigh registers 165°F, 1 to 1½ hours, depending on the heat of your grill.

While the bird is cooking, make the panzanella: Combine the bread, tomatoes, cucumbers, and onion in a large serving bowl. Drizzle the olive oil and vinegar over the salad, stirring or tossing to mix well. Season well with salt and pepper, tossing again. (The salad can be dressed up to 2 hours in advance and set aside at room temperature.) Just before serving, tear the basil leaves and scatter them over the salad, then toss again.

When the chicken is cooked, transfer to a carving board or large platter and let rest for 10 minutes.

Carve the chicken and arrange on a platter. Be sure to pour all the delicious juices over and around the chicken. Place the bunches of grapes around the chicken and serve with the panzanella.

Sometimes we brine chickens before roasting them, but it's unnecessary when spit-roasting, because the birds "self-baste" as they turn on the rotisserie. It's a great natural way of keeping in all the juices.

SPIT-ROASTED
GUINEA HENS
WITH VIN SANTO AND PRUNES

SERVES 4

2 large guinea hens (about 2 pounds each),
  livers reserved for another use if desired

  Kosher salt and freshly ground black pepper

18 fresh sage leaves

1 cup pitted prunes

1 cup chicken stock

½ cup vin santo

1 tablespoon tomato *conserva* or tomato paste

PREPARE A GAS OR CHARCOAL GRILL for rotisserie cooking over indirect medium heat (or according to the instructions for your grill). Set up the drip pan under the center of the spit.

Season the birds inside and out with salt and pepper. Stuff each one with 6 sage leaves and a prune. Tie the legs of each bird together with kitchen twine.

Place the hens on the spit and secure them with the clamps. Attach the spit to the rotisserie mechanism, cover the grill, and cook the hens until the thickest part of the thigh registers 165°F, about 45 minutes to 1 hour, depending on the heat of your grill.

Meanwhile, combine the remaining 6 sage leaves, the remaining prunes, the chicken stock, vin santo, and tomato *conserva* in a medium saucepan and bring to a simmer, stirring occasionally. Reduce the heat slightly and simmer for 30 minutes, stirring occasionally, to plump the prunes. Remove from the heat and set aside.

When the birds are cooked, transfer to a platter and let rest for 5 to 10 minutes, then cut them in half and serve with the prunes and some of their liquid.

As simple as it gets. The soft prune compote adds a kind of Moorish sweetness to this dish that I really love. Guinea hens can be on the lean side, but the natural self-basting that results when they are spit-roasted means there is considerably less chance of their drying out. Save the livers for crostini (see page 64) if you like. Serve the hens with the prunes and Sweet Potatoes in Cartoccio (page 229).

SPIT-ROASTED
TURKEY BREAST
PORCHETTA-STYLE

SERVES 8

¼ cup extra-virgin olive oil

1 pound sweet Italian sausages, removed from casings

1 medium onion, finely chopped

3 shallots, finely chopped

3 garlic cloves, minced

2 tablespoons fennel seeds

3 cups ½-inch cubes real bread

½ cup chicken broth

1 large egg

1 tablespoon chopped fresh thyme

1 teaspoon chopped fresh rosemary

Kosher salt and freshly ground black pepper

One 3- to 4-pound boneless turkey half breast

In a 10- to 12-inch sauté pan, combine 2 tablespoons of the oil and the sausages and cook over medium-high heat, stirring and breaking up the clumps of sausage, until all the pink is gone, about 5 minutes. Add the onion, shallots, garlic, and fennel seeds and cook until the onion and shallots are softened, about 5 minutes. Remove from the heat and allow to cool for about 10 minutes.

In a large bowl, toss the cubes of bread with the sautéed onion mixture, then add the chicken broth and toss to moisten all the bread. Add the egg, thyme, rosemary, and salt and pepper to taste and mix well. Cover the stuffing and refrigerate until completely cool.

Butterfly the turkey breast, leaving the skin on: Using a sharp knife, starting from the thinner long side, cut the breast horizontally in half almost but not all the way through, and open it up like a book. Pound it lightly with a meat mallet to even the thickness and shape. Season with salt and pepper and set aside on a platter.

Prepare a gas or charcoal grill for rotisserie cooking over indirect medium heat (or according to the instructions for your grill). Set up the drip pan under the center of the spit.

Cut 8 to 10 long pieces of kitchen twine. Spread the stuffing evenly over the turkey breast, leaving a 1-inch border on all sides. Starting from a long side, roll it up like a jelly roll and tie with the twine. Brush all over with the remaining 2 tablespoons olive oil.

Place the turkey breast on the spit and secure it with the clamps. Attach the spit to the rotisserie mechanism, cover the grill, and cook the turkey breast for 1 hour, or until the internal temperature in the thickest part reaches 155° to 160°F.

Transfer the turkey to a cutting board and let stand for 10 minutes before carving into generous slices.

Butterflying a boneless turkey breast is not difficult, but your butcher will be happy to do it for you if you show him or her this recipe. This porky version of roasted turkey will definitely change your expectations for turkey flavor forever. Be sure not to overcook the turkey, and let it rest so the juices are reabsorbed throughout the breast.

SPIT-ROASTED DUCK
WITH ORANGE AND ROSEMARY

SERVES 4

½ cup orange marmalade

½ cup fresh orange juice

3 tablespoons balsamic vinegar

4 garlic cloves, minced

2 tablespoons finely chopped fresh rosemary

One 4- to 4½-pound duck

Kosher salt and freshly ground black pepper

PREPARE A GAS OR CHARCOAL GRILL for rotisserie cooking over indirect medium heat (or according to the instructions for your grill). Set up the drip pan under the center of the spit.

In a small saucepan, combine the marmalade, orange juice, balsamic vinegar, garlic, and rosemary and bring to a boil. Reduce the heat and simmer for 5 minutes. Remove from the heat and let cool, then pour ¼ cup of the sauce into a small bowl to use for basting the duck, and pour the rest into a small serving bowl.

Meanwhile, remove all the excess fat from the duck. Wash and dry thoroughly both inside and out with paper towels. With a sharp metal skewer, prick the duck skin all over in 50 places, especially the thighs. Season inside and out with salt and pepper. Tie the legs together and brush all over with a light coating of the orange marmalade mixture.

Place the duck on the spit and secure it with the clamps. Attach it to the rotisserie mechanism, cover the grill, and cook until the temperature in the thickest part of the thigh reaches 160°F, 1¼ to 1¾ hours, depending on the heat of your grill. About 15 minutes before the duck is done, brush it all over again with more of the orange sauce. When the duck is done, transfer to a cutting board and let rest for 15 minutes.

Carve the duck and serve with the remaining orange sauce.

If you've only had oven-roasted duck, this recipe just may change your whole opinion of the bird. It comes out so crisp and delicious, with a deep brown burnished skin, it's almost like Chinese food duck. But to render the fat, you really have to prick the skin all over—fifty times, in fact (count 'em!).

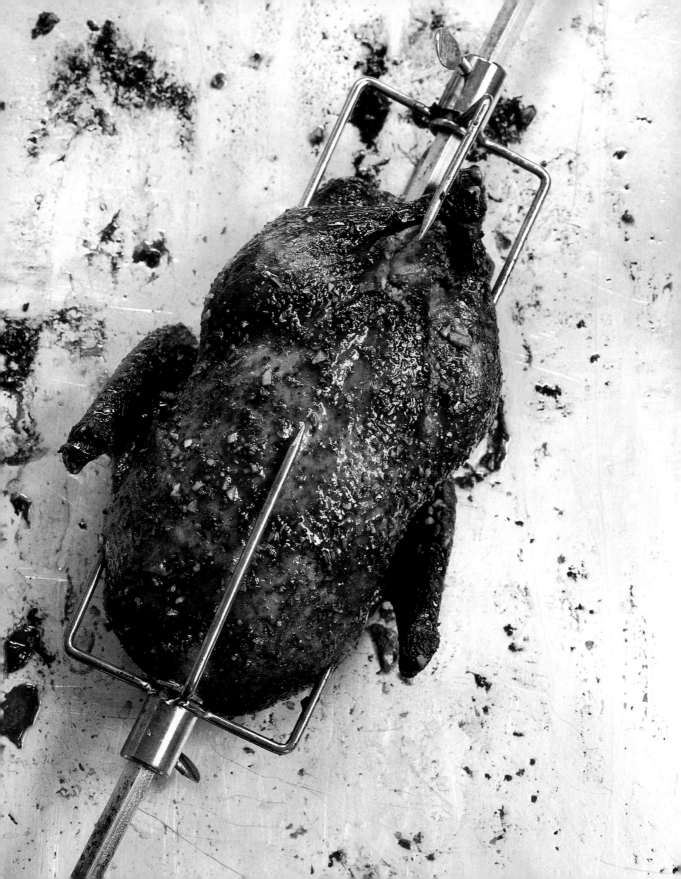

The sizzle, the fragrance, the promise of pleasure and deliciousness: American meat on a grill evokes a million memories and infinite potential whenever you hear it, smell it, and see it through that light veil of smoke anywhere. It is a nearly primordial sensation, universal among grillers everywhere. We all know there's nothing better than a grilled steak, and there's no better grilled steak than the Fiorentina, a big, thick T-bone traditionally served very rare,…unless it's the Tagliata of Bone-in Rib Eye. You will want to find a good butcher when you treat yourself and your guests to either of these steaks—but then why go back to the supermarket for any meat after that? No Italian cook buys meat that comes wrapped airtight in plastic on a little tray (which is a terrible way to treat meat in any case), and today we have many more markets with real meat departments again, with butchers who know all about what they are selling and will be happy to discuss it with you. And, if you haven't looked recently, you may be surprised to find that you can buy great meat at many greenmarkets—and can support your local farmers in the process. (But if you don't have access to either a farmers' market or a good butcher, you can order high-quality beef, pork, and lamb, including specialty cuts, online; see Sources, page 232.)

There are recipes here for when you want to indulge or celebrate, including the above-mentioned steaks; the Beef Braciole "Pinwheel-Style," a traditional homey dish turned elegant with beef tenderloin; Veal Chops with Flash-Pickled Mushrooms; and Grilled Arista-Style Pork Loin with Milk Sauce, a big bone-in roast seasoned with a Tuscan spice rub. But there are also dishes made with more economical, and very flavorful, cuts, including the Pork Shoulder Braciole, Ribs Italian-Style, and even an almost traditional Sausages and Peppers. You'll also find irresistible Grilled Lamb Chops Scottadita and two tasty recipes for leg of lamb: one butterflied and seasoned extravagantly with garlic and rosemary, the other spit-roasted and served with a mint pesto. And then there is one of my all-time favorite dishes, Fresh Ham alla Porchetta, perhaps the supreme achievement of spit-roasting.

T-BONE

FIORENTINA WITH SAUTÉED SPINACH

SERVES 4

HERB MIX

1 tablespoon chopped fresh rosemary

1 tablespoon chopped fresh sage

1 tablespoon fresh thyme leaves

2 tablespoons kosher salt

2 tablespoons freshly ground black pepper

One 3- to 3½-pound T-bone steak, about 3 inches thick

5 tablespoons extra-virgin olive oil

6 garlic cloves, thinly sliced

2 pounds trimmed baby spinach, washed and spun dry

Kosher salt

Grated zest of 1 lemon

Juice of ½ lemon, or more to taste

Freshly ground black pepper

Great extra-virgin olive oil for drizzling

Coarse sea salt

IN A SMALL BOWL, combine the rosemary, sage, thyme, salt, and pepper and mix well. Pat the steak dry and coat it all over with the herb mix. Drizzle 1 tablespoon of the olive oil over one side of the steak to moisten the herb mixture, and rub it gently into the mixture so it will adhere to the meat. Turn the steak over and repeat on the other side with another tablespoon of olive oil. Place on a plate, cover with plastic wrap, and let stand for 30 minutes to 1 hour to come to room temperature.

Meanwhile, preheat a gas grill or prepare a hot fire in a charcoal grill (use enough coals to keep the fire going for about 25 minutes).

Place the steak on the grill, cover the grill, and cook until the meat is well charred on the first side, 10 to 12 minutes. Turn and cook for 10 to 12 minutes on the second side, or until the internal temperature registers 120°F. Fiorentina is traditionally served rare; for medium-rare, cook until the center registers 125°F. Transfer to a carving board and let rest, uncovered, for 10 to 15 minutes.

Meanwhile, in a large heavy pot, heat the remaining 3 tablespoons olive oil over medium-high heat until very hot. Add the garlic and cook, stirring, just until golden. Add a few big handfuls of the spinach, sprinkle lightly with salt, and cook, stirring or turning with tongs, just until wilted. Add the remaining spinach in batches, lightly seasoning each batch and stirring or turning just until wilted. Remove from the heat and add the lemon zest, juice, and salt and pepper to taste.

Carve the fillet and the strip steak from the bone and slice the meat. Divide the steak among four plates, drizzle with olive oil, and sprinkle with coarse salt. Place the spinach next to the steak and serve immediately.

The Fiorentina, a big thick T-bone steak grilled and served rare, is one of the glories of Tuscan cooking. You will probably have to special-order the steak, which will be well worth it—and if you happen to have access to prime beef, now is the time to splurge. (For a different take on this dish, see Tuna Like Fiorentina, page 116.) Classic Tuscan beans would be nice with this— as would classic American potato salad.

TAGLIATA
OF BONE-IN RIB EYE WITH ARUGULA

SERVES 4

2 tablespoons sugar

1 tablespoon kosher salt

1 tablespoon freshly ground black pepper

1 tablespoon hot red pepper flakes

¼ cup porcini mushroom powder (see page 21)

5 garlic cloves, minced

¼ cup extra-virgin olive oil, plus about 1 tablespoon

One 3- to 3½-pound bone-in rib-eye steak, about 3 inches thick

3 cups trimmed arugula, washed and spun dry

Fine sea salt

Great extra-virgin olive oil for drizzling

Balsamic vinegar for drizzling

IN A SMALL BOWL, combine the sugar, salt, black pepper, red pepper flakes, mushroom powder, garlic, and ¼ cup olive oil and stir well to form a thick paste with the consistency of wet sand.

Rub the paste all over the steak, coating it evenly. Wrap tightly in plastic wrap and refrigerate for at least 12 hours, or overnight.

About 1 hour before grilling, remove the steak from the refrigerator and brush off the excess marinade with a paper towel. Place the steak on a plate and let come to room temperature.

Preheat a gas grill or prepare a fire in a charcoal grill (use enough coals to keep the fire going for about 25 minutes).

Put the steak on the hottest part of the grill, cover, and cook, turning every 6 to 8 minutes, for about 25 minutes for medium-rare; the internal temperature should be 125°F. Transfer to a carving board and let rest for 15 minutes.

Meanwhile, dress the arugula with about 1 tablespoon olive oil and season with sea salt to taste.

Slice the meat against the grain into ½-inch-thick pieces. Arrange on plates or a platter, drizzle with olive oil and balsamic vinegar, and top with the arugula. Serve immediately.

Rib eye is the steak they eat in Italy when they can't find the T-bone for Fiorentina. (The word *tagliata* merely refers to the fact that the steak is served sliced rather than whole.) The sugar in the spice crust helps develop the char and "steakhouse" crust you want, and the porcini powder adds an immeasurable earthy component. Make this for a celebration dinner.

BEEF BRACIOLE
"PINWHEEL-STYLE"

SERVES 6

2   garlic cloves, finely minced

4   scallions, thinly sliced

¼   cup chopped fresh Italian parsley

4   ounces thinly sliced salami, cut into ¼-inch-wide matchsticks

8   ounces Italian Fontina, cut into ¼-inch cubes

½   cup freshly grated Parmigiano-Reggiano

½   cup toasted bread crumbs

¼   cup plus 3 tablespoons extra-virgin olive oil

One 10-inch-long beef tenderloin roast cut from the heart of the tenderloin (2½ to 3 pounds), butterflied (see Note)

Kosher salt and freshly ground black pepper

IN A MEDIUM BOWL, combine the garlic, scallions, parsley, salami, Fontina, Parmigiano, and bread crumbs and mix well. Add ¼ cup of the olive oil and mix well with your hands or a spoon. Set aside.

Cut six 15-inch-long pieces of kitchen twine. Open out the beef, season on both sides with salt and pepper, and place it on a work surface so a long side is toward you. Spread the bread crumb mixture evenly over the beef, leaving a ½-inch border along the side farthest from you; press and gently pack the stuffing mixture onto the beef to keep it in place (you may have a little stuffing left over—it makes a great panini filling). Starting from the side nearest you, roll up the meat like a jelly roll, pressing any stuffing that falls out of the ends back into the roll, and tie tightly with the twine, spacing the ties evenly (it's easier if you have a

friend to tie the beef while you hold the roll together). Wrap tightly in plastic wrap to make a compact roll, and place in the refrigerator for at least 2 hours, or as long as overnight.

Preheat a gas grill or prepare a fire in a charcoal grill.

Carefully unwrap the beef roll and, using a very sharp knife, cut it between the ties into six thick pinwheels. Brush gently on both sides with the remaining 3 tablespoons olive oil and season with salt and pepper.

Gently lay the pinwheels on the hottest part of the grill and cook, unmoved, for 5 to 7 minutes. Using a spatula, carefully turn each pinwheel over and cook for about 4 minutes longer for medium-rare. (Don't be alarmed if some of the cheese in the stuffing starts to melt and char on the grill, making kind of a savory Florentine-cookie-like thing; but if you find it charring too much, move the pinwheels to a slightly cooler part of the grill.) Transfer to a platter and serve.

Note: To butterfly the beef, simply use a sharp knife to cut it horizontally almost but not all the way in half, starting from one of the long sides, so you can open it out like a book.

Beef braciole is traditionally made with slices of top round or a similar cut, pounded thin and wrapped around a savory filling, and it's a mainstay at street fairs. Here is a more refined version, all the lusty flavors of braciole wrapped up in a butterflied tenderloin—and the results are spectacular. You can have the butcher butterfly the meat, but it's easy to do yourself (see Note). Be sure to buy good salami for this dish, from an Italian market or, even better, from www.salumicuredmeats.com.

GRILLED LAMB CHOPS
SCOTTADITA

SERVES 6

Grated zest of 3 lemons

¼ cup coarsely chopped fresh mint, plus 4 whole sprigs for garnish

1 tablespoon sugar

Kosher salt and freshly ground black pepper

24 lamb rib chops (about 3½ pounds)

1 cup goat's-milk yogurt, such as Coach Farm

1 tablespoon cumin seeds, toasted and finely ground in a spice grinder

COMBINE TWO-THIRDS OF THE LEMON ZEST (reserve the rest for garnish), the chopped mint, sugar, and 1 teaspoon each salt and pepper in a food processor and process until the mixture has the texture of coarse sand.

Rub each chop well on both sides with a little of the mint mixture. Place on a baking sheet or platter, cover, and set aside at room temperature.

Preheat a gas grill or prepare a fire in a charcoal grill.

Combine the yogurt and cumin in a small bowl, blending well. Season with salt and pepper and transfer to a small serving bowl. Set aside.

Grill the chops, turning once, until medium-rare, about 2 minutes on each side. Pile the chops on a serving platter and garnish with the reserved lemon zest and the mint sprigs. Set out the cumin yogurt next to the platter, and serve immediately.

Loosely translated, *scottadita* means "burn your fingers," a reflection of the fact that these little chops are so irresistible you can't wait to start eating them. We usually cook them rare or medium-rare, but don't worry if you get distracted while you're tending them on the grill—even well-done, they are delicious. Scottadita is a classic Roman dish; the cumin yogurt adds a little bit of a North African touch, a nice foil for the mint-scented chops.

BUTTERFLIED
LEG OF LAMB
WITH GARLIC, ROSEMARY, AND MINT

SERVES 8

½ cup olive oil

½ cup vin santo

¼ cup chopped fresh mint

18 garlic cloves, peeled and bashed a bit with the side of a heavy knife

2 tablespoons kosher salt

1 tablespoon freshly ground black pepper

One 4½- to 5-pound boneless leg of lamb, butterflied and trimmed of excess fat (or one 7- to 8-pound bone-in leg, boned, butterflied, and trimmed)

2 tablespoons fresh rosemary leaves

COMBINE THE OLIVE OIL, vin santo, mint, 6 of the garlic cloves, the salt, and the pepper in a small bowl. Set aside.

Make 12 small incisions in the fatty side of the lamb and insert one of the remaining bashed garlic cloves and some of the rosemary into each slit. Put the lamb in a large baking dish and pour the marinade over, turning to coat. Let stand at cool room temperature for 1 hour, or cover and refrigerate for at least 12 hours, or overnight; turn the lamb occasionally as it marinates.

If the lamb has been in the refrigerator, bring it to room temperature. Preheat a gas grill or prepare a fire in a charcoal grill.

Remove the lamb from the marinade, draining it well, and pat dry. Pour the marinade into a small bowl. Place the lamb on the grill and cook, basting several times with the reserved marinade, for 10 to 12 minutes, until well charred on the first side. Turn and cook, basting several more times, for 10 to 12 minutes longer, or until well charred on the second side; the internal temperature should register 130°F for medium-rare. Transfer the lamb to a carving board and let it rest for 15 minutes.

Carve the lamb into ¼-inch-thick slices and serve immediately.

The vin santo in the marinade helps the meat develop a tasty char on the outside, like a steak. Cook it medium-rare, or even medium; unlike a butterflied beef tenderloin, for example, a butterflied leg of lamb always has some thicker and some thinner parts, which is actually a good thing—it means that when the meat is cooked, there will be something for everyone, some medium-rare, some medium, some a bit more done.

PORK TENDERLOIN
WITH JERUSALEM ARTICHOKES AND
NEGRONI VINAIGRETTTE

SERVES 6

½ cup porcini mushroom powder
(see page 21)

½ cup packed brown sugar

¼ cup hot red pepper flakes

3 tablespoons fennel seeds, coarsely crushed
in a spice or coffee grinder

3 large or 4 medium pork tenderloins (about 3
pounds total), trimmed of fat and silver skin

1 pound Jerusalem artichokes (sunchokes),
scrubbed

About 2½ cups kosher salt

1 pound haricots verts, trimmed

2 tablespoons extra-virgin olive oil

4 ounces pancetta, cut into ¼-inch cubes
(ask the butcher to slice the pancetta ¼ inch
thick when you buy it)

½ cup Negroni Vinaigrette (recipe follows)

Freshly ground black pepper

IN A SMALL BOWL, combine the porcini powder, brown sugar, red pepper flakes, and fennel seeds and stir well. Rub the mixture all over the pork tenderloins, coating the meat evenly. Wrap each tenderloin tightly in plastic wrap and refrigerate for at least 12 hours, or up to 24 hours.

Meanwhile, preheat the oven to 375°F.

Spread a thin layer of salt over the bottom of a small roasting pan or a baking dish that will hold the Jerusalem artichokes in a single layer. Arrange the artichokes in the pan and pour 2¼ cups salt, or enough to cover them completely, over and around them.

Roast the Jerusalem artichokes, uncovered, for 45 minutes, or until they are tender when pierced with a sharp knife. Remove the pan from the oven, carefully remove the artichokes from the salt with tongs, and set them aside on a plate to cool.

Brush the salt from the artichokes and slice them ¼ inch thick. Set aside. (The artichokes can be prepared up to 1 day ahead, covered, and refrigerated; bring to room temperature before proceeding.)

Bring a large pot of generously salted water to a boil. Set up an ice bath nearby. Add the haricots verts to the boiling water, bring back to a boil, and cook for 2 to 3 minutes, just until crisp-tender. Drain and immediately refresh in the ice bath. When the beans have cooled, drain again and set aside.

Unwrap the pork, brush off the excess rub, and set aside on a plate to come to room temperature.

Preheat a gas grill or prepare a fire in a charcoal grill.

Lightly oil the grill grate, using a clean rag dipped in oil or a basting brush. Place the tenderloins on the grill and cook, turning every 4 to 5 minutes, for 13 to 15 minutes, or until the center of the meat registers 130° to 135°F. Transfer the tenderloins to a platter and let rest for 10 minutes.

Meanwhile, in a deep 12- to 14-inch skillet or a large pot, heat the olive oil over medium heat. Add the pancetta, reduce the heat to medium-low, and cook, stirring frequently, until caramelized and golden brown, 5 to 7 minutes. Add the Jerusalem artichokes and the vinaigrette and toss over high heat for 2 to 3 minutes, until the artichokes are coated with the sauce and hot. Add the haricots verts and toss until coated and heated through. Season with salt if necessary and with pepper and remove from the heat.

Slice the tenderloins about ¼ inch thick. Arrange the Jerusalem artichokes and haricots verts on a platter and place the sliced pork on top. Drizzle with the sauce remaining in the pan and serve.

A classic Negroni is made with gin, sweet vermouth, and Campari (a type of Italian bitters) and garnished with an orange slice. Without the gin and with the addition of rosemary, the combination makes an unusual and mysteriously flavored saucy thing, which I use to glaze the vegetables served with the grilled spice-rubbed tenderloin. Roasting the Jerusalem artichokes in salt makes them very creamy inside; you can cook them early in the day or even the day before.

NEGRONI VINAIGRETTE
MAKES 1 CUP

1 cup sweet red vermouth, preferably Cinzano

¼ cup Campari

¼ cup fresh orange juice

¼ cup red wine vinegar

1 tablespoon fresh rosemary leaves

Kosher salt and freshly ground black pepper

¾ cup extra-virgin olive oil

IN A SMALL heavy saucepan, combine the vermouth, Campari, orange juice, vinegar, and rosemary and bring to a boil. Reduce the heat slightly and boil gently until the liquid is reduced to ¼ cup. Season with salt and pepper to taste, remove from the heat, and set aside to cool.

Strain the mixture into a medium bowl; discard the rosemary. Slowly whisk in the olive oil until emulsified and smooth; the vinaigrette will be fairly thick. Adjust the seasoning if necessary. (The vinaigrette can be stored in the refrigerator, covered, for up to 1 week; bring to room temperature before using.)

GRILLED ARISTA-STYLE PORK LOIN WITH MILK SAUCE

SERVES 6

3 tablespoons coarse sea salt or kosher salt

3 tablespoons sugar

3 tablespoons freshly ground black pepper

3 tablespoons ground fennel seeds

One 4-pound center-cut bone-in pork loin roast, chine bone removed by the butcher

8 small garlic cloves, lightly smashed

2 tablespoons extra-virgin olive oil

MILK SAUCE

¾ cup extra-virgin olive oil

12 garlic cloves

2 Spanish onions

1 fennel bulb

2 cups whole milk

1 tablespoon fennel seeds

1 teaspoon hot red pepper flakes

Kosher salt and freshly ground black pepper

COMBINE THE SALT, SUGAR, PEPPER, and ground fennel in a small bowl and mix well. Season the pork roast all over with the spice rub, massaging it into the meat and fat. Turn the roast bone side up and, with a thin sharp knife, make four 3-inch-deep incisions into the meat along the bones. Stuff 2 garlic cloves into each incision. Place the pork roast on a platter and let stand at room temperature for 30 minutes.

Prepare a gas or charcoal grill for indirect grilling.

Drizzle 1 tablespoon of the olive oil over one side of the pork roast to moisten the spice mixture, and rub it gently into the mixture so it will adhere to the meat. Turn the roast over and repeat on the other side with the remaining tablespoon of olive oil.

Place the roast on the cooler part of the grill, cover the grill, and cook for 1¾ to 2 hours, or until the internal temperature reaches 145° to 150°F. Transfer the roast to a carving board and allow to rest for 20 minutes.

While the roast cooks, make the sauce: Combine ¼ cup of the olive oil and the garlic in a medium pot and set over low heat. Halve the onions lengthwise, cut into ½-inch-thick slices, and add to the pot. Trim the fennel, reserving a few fronds for garnish. Cut the fennel lengthwise in half, then cut into ½-inch-thick slices and add to the pot. Increase the heat to medium-low and cook, stirring frequently, until the onions and fennel are very soft, about 15 minutes.

Add the milk, fennel seeds, and red pepper flakes to the pot and bring to a boil. Lower the heat and simmer until the onions and fennel are very tender, almost melting, 15 to 20 minutes. Remove from the heat and allow to cool slightly.

Transfer the onion mixture to a blender or food processor and puree until smooth. With the motor running, slowly drizzle in the remaining ½ cup olive oil until emulsified and smooth. Season to taste with salt and pepper.

Carve the pork loin off the bone. Cut the bones apart and put them on a platter for those who want to gnaw on them. Cut the pork loin into ½-inch-thick slices. Pour some of the sauce onto another platter and lay the slices of roast on top. Garnish with fennel fronds and serve with the remaining sauce in a sauceboat.

Arista (the name means "the best") is a celebratory Tuscan dish, sometimes made with a whole suckling pig studded with garlic and slowly spit-roasted. I like this garlicky pork loin roast, in the same spirit but a lot easier to do. Pork braised in milk is another regional classic, a specialty of Bologna. The milk used for braising becomes the sauce, and it's delicious, but it inevitably curdles—if you just zap the sauce (my version includes fennel too) quickly in the blender or food processor, though, it smooths out, and it's delicious.

PORK SHOULDER
BRACIOLE

SERVES 6

1½ cups toasted bread crumbs

4 ounces thinly sliced salami, cut into ¼-inch-wide matchsticks

½ cup freshly grated pecorino romano

1 bunch mint, leaves only, finely chopped

½ cup finely chopped fresh Italian parsley

Grated zest of 3 oranges

½ cup plus 2 tablespoons olive oil

Twelve ½-inch-thick slices boneless pork shoulder (about 2½ pounds)

Kosher salt and freshly ground black pepper

2 oranges, cut into wedges

COMBINE THE BREAD CRUMBS, salami, pecorino, mint, parsley, and orange zest in a large bowl and mix well. Add ½ cup of the olive oil and mix well with your hands or a spoon. Set aside.

Cut twenty-four 10-inch-long pieces of kitchen twine. Using a meat mallet, pound the pork pieces very thin. Season on both sides with salt and pepper. Spread a thin layer of stuffing (about ⅓ cup) on each slice of meat. Starting from a long side, roll each one up like a jelly roll and tie with 2 pieces of the twine, making a little packet. Place on a plate and refrigerate until ready to cook.

Preheat a gas grill or prepare a fire in a charcoal grill.

Brush the rolls lightly with the remaining 2 tablespoons olive oil and season with salt and pepper. Place the rolls over medium-high heat and cook, turning occasionally, until deeply marked with grill marks on all sides, about 15 minutes. Turn off one burner if using a gas grill, and move the rolls to the cooler part of the grill; or move them to the cooler perimeter of a charcoal grill. Cover the grill and cook, turning occasionally, for 20 to 25 minutes, or until the internal temperature is 185° to 190°F.

Transfer the rolls to a platter and serve with the orange wedges.

Another variation on braciole, the stuffed rolls of beef, or veal, or pork Italians like so much. The orange wedges provide the sweetness that goes so well with beautiful grilled pork. Buy the best salami you can find for this—such as my dad's (see www.salumicuredmeats.com).

PORK CHOPS
WITH PEPPERS AND CAPERS

SERVES 6

BRINE

4½ quarts water

1 cup kosher salt

1 cup packed brown sugar

12 black peppercorns

4 bay leaves

6 pork rib chops

3 tablespoons extra-virgin olive oil

3 red bell peppers, cored, seeded, and cut into thin strips

3 yellow bell peppers, cored, seeded, and cut into thin strips

8 bulb onions, trimmed and quartered, or 2 red onions, halved lengthwise and cut into ¼-inch-thick slices

¼ cup Gaeta olives, pitted and chopped

1 tablespoon hot red pepper flakes, or to taste

2 tablespoons small capers, with their brine

1 cup dry white wine

Kosher salt and freshly ground black pepper

IN A SMALL SAUCEPAN, combine 2 cups of the water, the salt, and brown sugar and heat over high heat, stirring, until the salt and sugar dissolve. Pour into a large deep bowl or another container large enough to hold the pork and the brine, add the peppercorns, the bay leaves, and the remaining 4 quarts cold water, and stir to mix well.

BRINING

Brining was originally used as a means of preserving meats and fish, but since the advent of refrigeration, such preservation techniques have been unnecessary. Yet brining has become popular again as a way of making meat, especially cuts that lack fat, and poultry succulent and tender. For more on the science of brining, see Harold McGee's *On Food and Cooking*, but essentially a light brine (not the salt-laden brine needed for long-term preserving) both tenderizes the meat and helps keep it moist during cooking. Water is the most common brining liquid, but beer, cider, or other liquids may be added, along with spices and herbs. Brines used for chicken and other poultry often contain sugar, which caramelizes during cooking and gives the skin of the bird a deep, rich golden brown color.

Make sure the brine is completely cool, then add the pork chops. Cover and refrigerate overnight.

The next day, heat the olive oil in a large pot over high heat until very hot. Add the peppers, onions, olives, red pepper flakes, and capers and cook, stirring, for 10 minutes, or until the peppers and onions are beginning to soften. Add the wine and bring to a boil, then lower the heat and simmer for 10 minutes. Season to taste with salt and pepper, remove from the heat, and set aside.

Preheat a gas grill or prepare a fire in a charcoal grill.

Drain the chops and pat dry with paper towels. Season on both sides with salt and pepper. Place the chops on the hottest part of the grill and cook for 7 minutes, unmoved. With tongs, carefully rotate the chops 90 degrees to create nice grill marks and cook for 4 minutes more. Turn the chops over and cook for 5 to 9 minutes more, or until the internal temperature is 145°F.

Transfer the chops to a platter, spoon the pepper mixture over, and serve.

We always use a brine for pork chops, and sometimes for larger cuts of pork as well. Brining the chops before grilling them guarantees succulent meat even when cooked to medium-well. The piquant and spicy combo of red and yellow peppers, red chili flakes, and capers makes this dish feel and taste like a bit of Little Italy.

ROSTICCIANA
(RIBS ITALIAN-STYLE)

SERVES 6

¼ cup paprika

3 tablespoons packed brown sugar

3 tablespoons salt

1 tablespoon ground cumin

6 garlic cloves, finely minced

10 bunches rosemary, soaked overnight in water to cover

3 large racks baby back ribs (about 2½ to 3 pounds per rack)

2 cups Mario's Kick-Ass Barbecue Sauce (recipe follows)

IN A SMALL BOWL, combine the paprika, brown sugar, salt, cumin, and garlic and mix well. Place the racks on a large baking sheet and rub generously on both sides with the spice mixture. Let stand for 2 hours at cool room temperature, or wrap in plastic and refrigerate for at least 6 hours, or up to 24 hours.

Prepare a gas grill for indirect grilling over low heat. Place a drip pan with an inch or so of water under the cool part of the grill. Pour about ⅔ cup of the barbecue sauce into a small bowl for basting, and pour the rest into a small serving bowl; refrigerate both bowls until about 30 minutes before serving.

Place the ribs on the cooler part of the grill, lay 1 bunch of wet rosemary on the hot part of the grill, and immediately cover the grill. (If your grill isn't large enough to arrange the 3 racks in a single layer for indirect cooking, place 2 of them on the grill and put the third one on top of them.) Cook the ribs for 5 hours; the temperature in the grill should be roughly 250°F. Every 30 minutes, place another bunch of wet rosemary on the hot part of the grill and immediately cover the grill to keep it smoky. Thirty minutes before the ribs are done, brush a light coating of barbecue sauce over them, and then repeat every 10 minutes.

Transfer the racks to a carving board and cut them into individual ribs. Serve with the remaining barbecue sauce.

These ribs are cooked "low and slow"—for five hours—but they are still juicy when they come off the grill. Stoking the grill with damp bunches of rosemary throughout the long cooking time creates the smoky environment of an outdoor smoker in a regular grill.

MARIO'S KICK-ASS
BARBECUE SAUCE

MAKES ABOUT 3 CUPS

1   medium onion, finely chopped

6   garlic cloves, finely chopped

2   cups ketchup

¾   cup fresh orange juice

¼   cup fresh lemon juice

¼   cup water

2   tablespoons red wine vinegar

2   tablespoons tomato paste

2   tablespoons honey

2   tablespoons packed brown sugar

2   tablespoons molasses

2   tablespoons Worcestershire sauce

2   tablespoons Dijon mustard

1   tablespoon chili powder

1   teaspoon ground cumin

1   teaspoon Tabasco or other hot sauce

COMBINE all the ingredients in a large heavy saucepan and bring to a boil over medium heat. Reduce the heat to low and simmer gently for 10 minutes, stirring frequently. Remove from the heat and let cool. (The sauce will keep for at least a week tightly covered in the refrigerator.)

This sauce works on almost anything, wherever you want a sweet spiked punch—eggs, chicken or other grilled meats, ham sandwiches, etc.

SAUSAGES
AND PEPPERS

SERVES 6

3 tablespoons olive oil

2 large red onions, cut into ½-inch chunks

3 large red bell peppers, cored, seeded, and cut into ½-inch squares

2 large yellow bell peppers, cored, seeded, and cut into ½-inch squares

1 large green bell pepper, cored, seeded, and cut into ½-inch squares

Kosher salt and freshly ground black pepper

1 fresh rosemary sprig

1 tablespoon balsamic vinegar

2 pounds sweet Italian sausages

5 or 6 fresh marjoram sprigs

PREHEAT A GAS GRILL or prepare a fire in a charcoal grill.

Heat the oil in a large heavy pot over medium heat. Add the onions, bell peppers, and salt and pepper to taste, then add the rosemary sprig and cook, stirring often, until the onions and peppers are very tender, 18 to 20 minutes. Add the balsamic vinegar and check the seasoning. Transfer to a large serving platter and set aside.

Using a sharp knife tip, prick each sausage seven or eight times. Place them on the grill, cover, and cook, turning them occasionally with tongs and moving them around as necessary when flare-ups occur, until cooked through, 12 to 15 minutes.

Arrange the sausages on top of the peppers. Pull the marjoram leaves from the sprigs, strew them over the sausages, and serve immediately.

A street-fair standby, in a slightly more refined version (although the sliced sausages and the peppers would still make a great sub filling). The quality of the sausages is paramount—find an artisanal butcher or someone who's using something different from the standard pork mix, and you will be rewarded.

VEAL CHOPS
WITH FLASH-PICKLED MUSHROOMS

SERVES 4

2 large heads garlic

4 large veal loin chops (about 12 to 14 ounces each)

5 tablespoons extra-virgin olive oil

4 shallots, finely chopped

1½ pounds chanterelles, brushed clean and halved

¾ cup red wine vinegar

Scant 1 tablespoon chopped fresh thyme

Kosher salt and freshly ground black pepper

PREHEAT THE OVEN TO 350°F.

Slice off the top ⅓ inch of each garlic head, exposing the cloves. Wrap the heads individually in foil and roast for 50 minutes to 1 hour, until the cloves are soft but not mushy. Let cool, then separate the garlic cloves and peel. Set aside. (The garlic can be prepared up to 1 day ahead and refrigerated.)

Remove the veal chops from the refrigerator to come to room temperature. Preheat a gas grill or prepare a fire in a charcoal grill.

In a large pot, heat 3 tablespoons of the olive oil over medium-high heat until almost smoking. Add the shallots and cook, stirring occasionally, until golden, 2 to 3 minutes. Add the mushrooms, reduce the heat to medium, and cook, stirring occasionally, until golden brown and slightly crispy, 8 to 10 minutes. Add the garlic cloves and vinegar and cook until the liquid is reduced to about ¼ cup. Stir in the thyme and season with salt and pepper. Remove from the heat and set aside.

Season the chops with salt and pepper and brush them with the remaining 2 tablespoons olive oil. Place on the hottest part of the grill and cook, turning once, for about 8 minutes per side for medium-rare. Transfer to a platter and let rest for 5 minutes.

Meanwhile, reheat the mushrooms over medium heat, stirring occasionally.

Spoon the mushrooms and sauce over and around the chops, and serve immediately.

Big veal loin chops are a real treat, and this simple but elegant dish is worthy of a special dinner. If chanterelles are not in season, substitute other wild mushrooms or even cremini (adjust the cooking time accordingly).

SPIT-ROASTED
PRIME RIB

SERVES 10

3 tablespoons kosher salt

3 tablespoons freshly ground black pepper

2 tablespoons finely chopped fresh rosemary, plus 2 or 3 whole sprigs

2 tablespoons fresh thyme leaves

2 tablespoons Colman's dry mustard

One 8-pound prime rib roast, chine bone removed and fat trimmed to a thin layer by the butcher

About 1 cup dry white wine

Coarse sea salt

IN A SMALL BOWL, combine the salt, pepper, chopped rosemary, thyme, and dry mustard and mix well. Rub the spice mixture generously all over the meat. Cover with plastic wrap and let stand for 1 hour at room temperature.

Prepare a gas or charcoal grill for spit-roasting over indirect medium heat (or according to the instructions for your grill). Pour about ½ inch of wine into the drip pan, add the rosemary sprigs, and set under the center of the spit.

Push the spit through the roast and secure it with the clamps. Attach the spit to the rotisserie mechanism, cover the grill, and cook for about 1½ to 2 hours, depending on the temperature of your grill, or until the internal temperature—insert an instant-read thermometer about 3 inches deep into the center of the roast, without touching the bones—reaches 115° to 120°F for medium-rare (the temperature will rise at least 5 degrees while the roast rests). Check the temperature after 1¼ hours, and once it has reached 110°F or so, check it often.

Remove the spit from the grill and place the roast, still on the spit, on a carving board (if you remove the spit before letting the roast rest, you will lose a lot of the juices) to rest for 15 to 20 minutes.

Remove the spit from the roast. Carve the roast off the bone and cut into ¾-inch-thick slices. Place on a platter, set out a small bowl of coarse salt and a pepper mill alongside, and serve.

This is the most dramatic dish in my canon of grill recipes. When it's properly cooked, you are heroic; if it's overcooked, you are a dog—so be careful, and use a thermometer to check the temperature. Serve with Sweet Potatoes *in Cartoccio* (page 229), Asparagus Wrapped in Pancetta with Citronette (page 30), and/or Thousand-Ridges Japanese Eggplant (page 213).

SPIT-ROASTED LEG OF LAMB WITH MINT PESTO

SERVES 8

One 4½- to 5-pound boneless leg of lamb, rolled and tied (or one 7- to 8-pound bone-in leg, boned, rolled, and tied)

6 garlic cloves

½ cup fresh lemon juice

¼ cup distilled white vinegar

1½ teaspoons balsamic vinegar

¼ cup extra-virgin olive oil

2 tablespoons chopped fresh Italian parsley

½ teaspoon paprika

½ teaspoon curry powder

1½ teaspoons freshly ground black pepper

Mint Pesto (recipe follows)

USING A THIN SHARP KNIFE, cut 6 deep slits in the lamb and insert a garlic clove into each hole. Put the lamb in a baking dish or large shallow bowl.

Combine the lemon juice, vinegars, olive oil, parsley, paprika, curry powder, and pepper in a small bowl, mixing well. Pour the marinade over the lamb and turn to coat. Cover and refrigerate for 6 to 8 hours, turning the lamb in the marinade every hour.

MINT PESTO

MAKES ABOUT 1 CUP

3 garlic cloves

2 cups lightly packed fresh mint leaves

3 tablespoons pine nuts

100 mg ascorbic acid (vitamin C), crushed

Generous pinch of kosher salt

½ cup plus 2 tablespoons extra-virgin olive oil

¼ cup freshly grated Parmigiano-Reggiano

3 tablespoons freshly grated pecorino romano

Forty-five minutes to an hour before you are ready to grill, remove the lamb from the refrigerator to allow it to come to room temperature.

Prepare a gas or charcoal grill for spit-roasting over indirect medium heat (or according to the instructions for your grill). Set up the drip pan under the center of the spit.

Remove the lamb from the marinade and pat dry; pour the marinade into a small bowl. Place the lamb on the spit and secure it with the clamps. Attach the spit to the rotisserie mechanism, cover the grill, and cook the lamb, basting it with the reserved marinade every 30 minutes, for 1¾ to 2 hours, or until the internal temperature reaches 130° to 140°F. Transfer the lamb to a carving board and allow to rest for 15 minutes.

Cut the lamb into thin slices and serve with the pesto.

WITH THE motor running, drop the the garlic into a food processor to chop it. Add the mint, pine nuts, ascorbic acid, and salt and pulse until the mint is coarsely chopped, then process until the mint and pine nuts are finely chopped. With the motor running, drizzle in the oil. Transfer to a small bowl and stir in the Parmigiano and pecorino. (The pesto can be stored in a tightly sealed jar, topped with a thin layer of extra-virgin olive oil, for several weeks in the refrigerator.)

Note: The ascorbic acid keeps the pesto from darkening.

When this is cooking in your backyard, be prepared for the entire neighborhood to come running over like starving hounds. The smoky fragrance from the grill is exactly what I find at grill restaurants in Toscana on Sundays all summer long. Make sure the butcher trims all the excess fat from the leg of lamb when he or she prepares it for you.

SPIT-ROASTED
FRESH HAM
ALLA PORCHETTA

SERVES 10, WITH LEFTOVERS FOR SANDWICHES

BRINE

1½ gallons water

5½ cups kosher salt

6 cups packed brown sugar

¼ cup fennel seeds

¾ cup crushed black peppercorns

One 6- to 8-pound bone-in leg of pork (shank end)

1 cup fresh sage leaves

12 garlic cloves

¼ cup fennel pollen or ground toasted fennel seeds

3 tablespoons kosher salt

2 tablespoons freshly ground black pepper

¼ cup extra-virgin olive oil

GLAZE

1 cup packed brown sugar

¼ cup plus 2 tablespoons apple cider vinegar

1 tablespoon Colman's dry mustard

2 tablespoons fennel seeds

COMBINE 3 QUARTS OF THE WATER, the salt, and the brown sugar in a large pot and heat over high heat, stirring, until the salt and sugar dissolve. Remove from the heat and pour into a large pot or other container large enough to hold the pork and the brine. Add the fennel seeds and peppercorns, and let cool completely.

Using a very sharp serrated knife or another sharp knife, score a series of parallel lines 1 inch apart in the skin of the ham, making them about ¼ inch deep. Then score another series of parallel lines diagonally across the first cuts to make a diamond crosshatch pattern. (Scoring the skin will make it crispy and delicious on the surface and succulent within.)

Add the remaining 3 quarts cold water to the salt and sugar mixture. Submerge the ham in the brine (weight it if necessary to keep it submerged) and refrigerate for 24 hours.

Remove the ham from the brine, rinse it well, and pat dry with paper towels. Set it on a platter to air-dry at room temperature for 1 hour.

Prepare a gas grill for spit-roasting over indirect medium heat (or according to the instructions for your grill). Set up the drip pan under the center of the spit.

Combine the sage, garlic, fennel pollen, salt, pepper, and olive oil in a food processor and process to a coarse paste. Rub this mixture into the nooks and crannies in the surface of the ham.

Place the roast on the spit and secure it with the clamps. Attach the spit to the rotisserie mechanism, cover the grill, and cook the ham for about 3 hours, or until the internal temperature reaches 150°F.

Meanwhile, for the glaze, combine the brown sugar, cider vinegar, mustard, and fennel seeds in a medium saucepan and bring to a boil, stirring to dissolve the sugar. Reduce the heat and simmer until reduced to about ¾ cup and syrupy. Pour into a bowl and set aside.

When the pork has reached 150°F, brush on a thin layer of the glaze. Continue cooking, brushing with the glaze two more times, until the internal temperature reaches 160°F. Transfer the pork to a carving board and allow to rest for 30 minutes before carving and serving.

I make this all the time—it's what spit-roasting was invented for. *Alla porchetta* refers to the great regional specialty made with a whole suckling pig, boned and flavored with garlic and rosemary or other herbs, including wild fennel. Porchetta is the centerpiece of many Italian festivals and other celebrations, but it is also served from street carts and market stalls, sliced to order for a casual snack or a sandwich.

VEGETABLES

Vegetables are treated with reverence in Italy, and in restaurants, *contorni* are served as a separate course, not as a secondary player overshadowed by the main dish. At home, the vegetables are more likely to accompany the main dish, as they do here. But for both restaurant chefs and home cooks, seasonality is the key, and I suggest that you, like them (and me), view the first step in cooking vegetables—the shopping—as the most important one. Shop at a farmers' market or farm stand whenever you can, and buy local, preferably organic, produce whenever possible. Sure, you can get asparagus in January and raspberries in November, but if you try to respect the seasons, you will truly be rewarded.

Italians almost always prepare vegetables simply, so the fennel, or the eggplant, or the red pepper tastes like itself. The recipes in this chapter reflect the same philosophy, offering simply grilled vegetables that may be marinated or simply finished with a drizzle of vinaigrette. And grilling can somehow bring out the essence of a vegetable, emphasizing the underlying smokiness in eggplant, whether in Thousand-Ridges Japanese Eggplant or Eggplant Parmigiana Packets, or caramelizing the natural sugars in Thick-Sliced Onions with Lemon Thyme. Grilled Porcini with Vin Cotto is one of the most extravagant recipes in the book and one of the simplest—if you start with fresh porcini, it is a criminal act to do much more than brush them with garlic-scented oil and toss them (gently) onto the grill just until golden brown and tender. Asparagus with Lemon-Prosciutto Vinaigrette, Scallions with Almond Pesto, and Grilled Artichokes with Mint and Chilies are all elegant dishes too—because of their main ingredient, not because of some fussy technique or preparation. And Corn as Italians Would Eat It may be wildly inauthentic, but it's fun and delicious, and nobody you know will be able to resist it.

GRILLED PORCINI
WITH VIN COTTO

SERVES 6

¼ cup plus 2 tablespoons extra-virgin olive oil

2 garlic cloves, thinly sliced

¼ cup chopped fresh Italian parsley

6 large porcini mushrooms, brushed clean and cut lengthwise in half

Kosher salt and freshly ground black pepper

Vin cotto for drizzling

PREHEAT A GAS GRILL or prepare a fire in a charcoal grill.

In a small bowl, combine the olive oil, garlic, and parsley. Brush the mushrooms on both sides with the oil and place cut side down on the grill over medium-high heat. Cook, turning occasionally and brushing with any remaining garlic oil, until golden brown and softened, about 10 minutes.

Arrange the porcini on a platter, drizzle lightly with vin cotto, and serve immediately.

Porcini, also called cèpes, are considered the king of wild mushrooms, and justifiably so. The best fresh porcini come from Italy, and they are now being imported here. (Their Italian name translates literally as "little piglets" and is fancifully derived from their squat round stems and shape.) If you are lucky enough to come across fresh porcini when they are in season in the spring and fall, treat yourself to this dish. But if your budget doesn't extend to such extravagance, you can substitute portobellos (use only the caps of 6 large mushrooms) or even puffballs, cut into 1-inch-thick slices.

EGGPLANT
PARMIGIANA PACKETS

SERVES 6

2 medium eggplant

About 5 tablespoons extra-virgin olive oil

¾ cup toasted bread crumbs

2 teaspoons chopped fresh thyme

¾ cup Basic Tomato Sauce (page 50)

½ cup freshly grated Parmigiano-Reggiano

8 ounces fresh mozzarella, cut into 12 thin slices

12 fresh basil leaves, cut into chiffonade (thin slivers)

PREHEAT A GAS GRILL or prepare a fire in a charcoal grill.

Trim the eggplant and cut lengthwise into ¼-inch-thick slices, discarding the first and last slices from each one; you should have 12 slices. Lay the slices on a baking sheet and lightly brush on both sides with olive oil, using about 3 tablespoons oil. Place on the grill and cook, turning once, until golden brown and soft, about 2 minutes on each side; return the slices to the baking sheet as they are cooked.

In a small bowl, combine the bread crumbs, thyme, and tomato sauce. Lay the eggplant slices out on a work surface, with a narrow end toward you. Divide the bread crumb mixture among them, using a scant ¼ cup for each and placing it on the lower half of each one. Sprinkle with the grated Parmigiano and lay the slices of mozzarella on top. Fold the tops of the eggplant slices over to create little packages and transfer to a clean baking sheet. Refrigerate for at least 1 hour, or as long as overnight, to marry the flavors.

Preheat the gas grill again or prepare another fire in the charcoal grill.

Carefully brush the eggplant packets on both sides with the remaining 2 tablespoons olive oil. Place them gently on the hottest part of the grill and cook, unmoved, for 2 minutes, or until nice grill marks appear on the first side. Gently flip over with a large spatula and cook for 2 more minutes, or until marked on the second side and hot throughout.

Carefully transfer the packets to a platter and sprinkle with the basil. Serve hot or at room temperature.

Grilling eggplant brings out its smoky flavor, and it requires far less oil than frying, making this a much lighter version than the all-too-typical tired eggplant Parm. Serve hot or at room temperature, two little packets per person.

ASPARAGUS

WITH LEMON-PROSCIUTTO VINAIGRETTE

SERVES 6

2 pounds jumbo asparagus, tough bottom stalks snapped off

Grated zest and juice of 2 lemons

½ cup extra-virgin olive oil

2 garlic cloves, minced

1½ teaspoons dried dill

Kosher salt and freshly ground black pepper

1 tablespoon red wine vinegar

2 ounces thinly sliced prosciutto di Parma, cut into julienne strips

PLACE THE ASPARAGUS in a baking dish large enough to hold it in no more than two layers. In a small bowl, combine the lemon zest and juice, olive oil, garlic, and dill and mix well. Pour over the asparagus, turning to coat. Set aside to marinate for at least 1 hour (or up to 6 hours), turning frequently.

Preheat a gas grill or prepare a fire in a charcoal grill.

Remove the asparagus from the marinade, draining it well; reserve the marinade. Working with groups of 3 spears each, skewer the asparagus with toothpicks: Place the spears side by side and run one toothpick through the stalks just under the tips and another one about 1 inch up from the bottoms. Season the asparagus on both sides with salt and pepper and set on a platter. (You can skewer the asparagus ahead and return it to the marinade until ready to cook; drain well again, reserving the marinade, before grilling.)

Pour the marinade into a small bowl and whisk in the vinegar, then stir in the prosciutto. Set aside.

Place the asparagus on the hottest part of the grill and cook until lightly charred on the first side, 3 to 5 minutes. Turn and cook until just tender, 2 to 3 minutes longer.

Place the asparagus on a platter, slipping out the toothpicks from each bunch as you do so. Stir the marinade again and pour it over the asparagus, using a fork to arrange the prosciutto attractively over the spears. Serve hot.

I love plain asparagus as much as anyone, but when you are serving a simple main course like Spit-Roasted Guinea Hens (page 154), a little sexiness in the *contorno* department makes it look as if you did a lot more work than you really did!

THOUSAND-RIDGES JAPANESE
EGGPLANT

SERVES 6

6 Japanese eggplant (about 2 pounds)

¼ cup olive oil

4 garlic cloves, finely minced

3 tablespoons finely chopped fresh oregano

Kosher salt and freshly ground black pepper

PREHEAT A GAS GRILL or prepare a fire in a charcoal grill.

Split each eggplant lengthwise in half. With a sharp knife, score the cut surface of each half with a series of parallel cuts on the diagonal about ¼ inch apart. Make a second series of cuts in the opposite direction to form a cross-hatch pattern.

Combine the olive oil, garlic, and oregano in a small bowl. Rub the cut surfaces of the eggplant halves with the olive oil mixture, coating them well, and season with salt and pepper.

Lay the eggplant halves cut side down on the grill and cook, unmoved, for 5 minutes, or until lightly browned and beginning to soften. Gently turn over and cook for 2 to 3 minutes more, or until softened. Transfer to a platter and serve.

Japanese eggplant is smaller and thinner than regular eggplant, ranging from pale lavender to deep violet in color. The skin is thinner, too, and sweeter, and the flesh is delicate, even creamy.

BUTTERNUT SQUASH
WITH VIN COTTO

SERVES 6

1   medium butternut squash (1½ to 2 pounds)

½   cup extra-virgin olive oil

¼   cup red wine vinegar

3   tablespoons honey

1   tablespoon chopped fresh rosemary

4   garlic cloves, finely minced

Kosher salt

Vin cotto for drizzling

CUT OFF THE NECK PORTION of the squash and cut it into ¼-inch-thick slices. Cut the bulb portion lengthwise in half, remove the seeds and membranes, and cut into ¼-inch-thick slices.

Combine the olive oil, vinegar, honey, rosemary, and garlic in a small bowl and mix well. Put the squash in a large baking dish or shallow bowl and pour the marinade over, turning to coat. Allow to stand for 2 hours at room temperature, or cover and refrigerate for as long as overnight, turning the squash occasionally.

Preheat a gas grill or prepare a fire in a charcoal grill.

Remove the squash from the marinade, draining well, and arrange in a single layer on one or two baking sheets; reserve the marinade. Season the squash on both sides with salt.

Arrange the squash on the grill (you will probably have to cook it in two batches) and cook until golden brown on the first side, 5 to 6 minutes. Turn and cook until browned on the second side and tender, about 5 minutes (the half-rings may take slightly less time than the whole slices). Transfer to a serving platter and drizzle with some of the reserved marinade. Cover with foil and let stand for 10 minutes.

Remove the foil, drizzle the squash with vin cotto, and serve.

Although it's considered a winter squash, butternut is now available almost year-round. I particularly love it right when it comes into its real season, mid- to late September, about the same time that tomatoes are at their best for me. Marinating the sliced squash in olive oil and red wine vinegar with fresh rosemary and then cooking it on the grill makes a delicious and different late-summer dish.

SCALLIONS
WITH ALMOND PESTO

SERVES 6

4 bunches scallions, trimmed (leave about 3 inches of the dark green parts)

About ½ cup Almond Pesto

2 lemons, cut into wedges

Coarse sea salt

PREHEAT A GAS GRILL or prepare a fire in a charcoal grill.

Lay the scallions over the hottest part of the grill and cook for 2 to 3 minutes, or until lightly charred on the first side. Turn and cook for 2 to 3 minutes more, until lightly charred on the second side. Transfer to a platter.

Spoon the pesto generously over the white parts of the scallions and serve hot, with the lemon wedges and coarse sea salt.

Grilled scallions are great, but they are often treated as a mere garnish. These are very reminiscent of a Catalonian dish of overwintered leeks called *calcots*. The almond pesto is a variation on the *romesco* sauce traditionally served with *calcots*.

ALMOND PESTO

MAKES ABOUT 1 CUP

2 garlic cloves

1 cup packed fresh Italian parsley leaves

2 teaspoons fresh thyme leaves, preferably lemon thyme

⅓ cup toasted unblanched almonds

Generous pinch of kosher salt

½ cup plus 2 tablespoons extra-virgin olive oil

¼ cup freshly grated Parmigiano-Reggiano

WITH THE MOTOR RUNNING, drop the the garlic into a food processor to chop it. Add the parsley, thyme, almonds, and salt and pulse until the herbs and nuts are coarsely chopped, then process until finely chopped. With the motor running, gradually drizzle in the oil. Transfer to a small bowl and stir in the Parmigiano.

THICK-SLICED ONIONS
WITH LEMON THYME

SERVES 6

¼ cup balsamic vinegar

2 garlic cloves, finely minced

3 tablespoons chopped fresh lemon thyme

2 pounds medium to large red onions

About ½ cup extra-virgin olive oil

Kosher salt and freshly ground black pepper

PREHEAT A GAS GRILL or prepare a fire in a charcoal grill.

Combine the vinegar, garlic, and thyme in a small saucepan and heat until fragrant and just beginning to steam (the mixture will register about 150°F on an instant-read thermometer); don't let it boil. Remove from the heat and let stand for 20 minutes.

Meanwhile, cut the onions into ½-inch-thick slices and lay out on a baking sheet. (To make it easier to turn the onions on the grill, and to avoid losing any onion rings in the fire, insert a toothpick into the side of each slice, pushing it halfway through; or put a wire cooling rack on the grill so the onions won't slip through.) Brush on both sides with 3 to 4 tablespoons of the olive oil and season with salt and pepper.

Place the onions on the hottest part of the grill and cook, unmoved, for 4 to 5 minutes, until just charred on the first side. Turn and cook for 3 to 4 minutes more, or until softened and lightly charred on the second side. Transfer to a baking sheet or platter and remove the toothpicks if you used them, then carefully stack the onion slices—like pancakes—on a serving platter.

Whisk the remaining ¼ cup olive oil into the vinegar mixture and drizzle it over the onions. Serve warm or at room temperature.

These are so good—grilling onions caramelizes the natural sugars and brings out all their inherent sweetness, which is emphasized in this dish by the balsamic in the vinaigrette. If you can only find regular thyme, whisk in some grated lemon zest along with the olive oil before drizzling the mixture over the onions.

CORN
AS ITALIANS WOULD EAT IT

MAKES 6 EARS

6 ears corn, shucked

¼ cup extra-virgin olive oil

3 tablespoons balsamic vinegar

1 to 1½ cups freshly grated
   Parmigiano-Reggiano

   About 2 tablespoons chopped fresh mint

   Hot red pepper flakes

PREHEAT A GAS GRILL or prepare a fire in a charcoal grill.

Place the corn on the hottest part of the grill and cook for 3 minutes, or until grill marks appear on the first side. Roll each ear over a quarter turn and cook for 2 to 3 minutes, then repeat two more times.

Meanwhile, mix the oil and vinegar on a large flat plate. Spread the Parmigiano on another flat plate.

When the corn is cooked, roll each ear in the olive oil and vinegar mixture, shake off the extra liquid, and dredge in the Parmigiano to coat lightly. Place on a platter, sprinkle with the mint and pepper flakes, and serve immediately.

In Mexico, I have seen groovy little stands where the vendors poach ears of corn and then paint it with mayonnaise, dust it with chili flakes and grated *queso fresco*, and squeeze lime juice all over the whole thing. They do not do that in Italy, but this is what they might do. It's fantastic.

GRILLED ARTICHOKES
WITH MINT AND CHILIES

SERVES 6

6 large artichokes, preferably with stems

2 lemons, halved

1 bunch mint, chopped, stems and all, plus about ¼ cup fresh mint leaves cut into chiffonade (thin slivers)

6 garlic cloves, thinly sliced

1 cup extra-virgin olive oil

1 cup dry white wine

2 to 4 red jalapeños, diced or thinly sliced

Coarse sea salt

FILL A LARGE BOWL with about 6 cups of water and add the juice of 1½ of the lemons; add the 3 lemon halves too. Snap off the tough outer leaves from one artichoke until you come to the leaves that are pale yellow toward the bottom. Cut off the top 1 inch of the leaves. As you work, rub the cut surfaces with the remaining lemon half. Trim off the bottom of the stem and, using a paring knife, trim away the tough outer layer from the stem. Trim any dark green parts from the bottom of the artichoke. Halve the artichoke lengthwise and, using a grapefruit spoon or small sharp spoon, remove the fuzzy choke. Pull out the small purple inner leaves. Put the trimmed artichoke in the bowl of lemon water, and repeat with the remaining artichokes.

Combine the chopped mint, garlic, olive oil, and wine in a large pot. Add the artichokes and the lemon water, along with the lemon shells, then add more water if necessary to cover the artichokes. Put a pan lid on top of the artichokes to keep them submerged and bring to a boil over high heat. Reduce the heat, cover, and simmer until just tender, 15 to 20 minutes, depending on the size of the artichokes. Drain and allow to cool.

Preheat a gas grill or prepare a fire in a charcoal grill.

Place the artichokes cut side down over the hottest part of the grill and cook, unmoved, for 3 to 5 minutes, until nicely charred. Turn and cook for 5 minutes more, or until golden brown on the second side.

Place the artichokes on a platter and strew with the remaining mint and the jalapeños. Serve with a bowl of coarse salt.

You can prep and blanch the artichokes early in the day, then just toss them onto the grill and serve hot, sprinkled with the mint and diced red jalapeños.

ENDIVE

WITH MARJORAM AND PROVATURA

SERVES 6

¼ cup extra-virgin olive oil

Grated zest and juice of 1 lemon

Kosher salt and cracked black pepper

6 Belgian endive

2 to 3 tablespoons chopped fresh marjoram

A 4-ounce chunk of provatura or young provolone cheese for shaving

PREHEAT A GAS GRILL or prepare a fire in a charcoal grill.

Combine the olive oil, lemon zest and juice, and salt and pepper to taste (season aggressively) in a large bowl and mix well.

Cut the endive in half and toss gently in the oil mixture to coat. Drain well and place cut side down on the grill. Cook until soft and beginning to brown at the tips, about 6 to 8 minutes.

Transfer the endive to a platter, cut side up, and sprinkle with the marjoram. Shave the cheese over and serve.

With its slightly bitter edge, endive is very good when grilled. Provatura is a buffalo-milk cheese somewhat similiar to mozzarella. It's available in some Italian markets or good cheese shops, but a good young Italian provolone will also work well here.

SWEET POTATOES IN CARTOCCIO

SERVES 6

6 medium sweet potatoes, peeled and sliced ¼ inch thick

1 large Spanish onion, thinly sliced and separated into rings

¼ cup plus 2 tablespoons extra-virgin olive oil

Kosher salt and freshly ground black pepper

6 tablespoons (¾ stick) butter, softened

¼ cup plus 2 tablespoons packed light brown sugar

PREHEAT A GAS GRILL or prepare a fire in a charcoal grill.

Cut six 14-by-12-inch sheets of heavy-duty foil and lay them out on a work surface, with a short end toward you. Layer one-sixth of the potato slices and onion rings on the bottom half of each sheet of foil, leaving an inch or so of space all around. Brush the tops and sides of the vegetables with olive oil, using 1 tablespoon for each packet, and sprinkle with salt and pepper. Dot the top of each pile of potatoes with 1 tablespoon of the butter and sprinkle with 1 tablespoon of the brown sugar. Fold the foil over the squash, fold over about ¼ inch of the sides and bottoms of the foil to seal the edges, then fold over again to make a tight seal.

Place the packets on the hottest part of the grill and cook for 15 minutes. Transfer to a large platter or baking sheet and let stand for 10 minutes.

Serve in the foil, warning your guests about the hot, fragrant steam that will arise when they cut into the packets. Be sure to spoon some of the syrupy juices over the sweet potatoes.

The brown sugar and butter are here, but slicing sweet potatoes and cooking them *in cartoccio* with onions and olive oil gives them a whole new lease on life. Serve these with the Spit-Roasted Prime Rib (page 196) or Spit-Roasted Turkey Breast Porchetta-Style (page 156).

WAXY POTATOES
IN CHIANTI VINEGAR

SERVES 6

2 pounds small waxy potatoes, such as Yukon Gold or Ruby Crescent

¾ cup extra-virgin olive oil

1 tablespoon celery seeds

6 scallions, thinly sliced

2 tablespoons Dijon mustard

¼ cup Chianti vinegar or other good red wine vinegar

Kosher salt and freshly ground black pepper

IF USING WOODEN SKEWERS, soak them in water for at least 30 minutes.

Meanwhile, bring a large pot of salted water to a boil. Add the potatoes, bring back to a boil, and cook for 6 minutes. Drain and let cool slightly.

While the potatoes cook, preheat a gas grill or prepare a fire in a charcoal grill.

Cut the potatoes into 3 or 4 slices each. Combine ¼ cup of the olive oil, the celery seeds, and one-third of the scallions in a large bowl. Toss in the potatoes and turn or stir gently to coat.

Thread the potatoes onto 12 skewers (the easiest way to do this is line up 5 or so potato slices at a time, cut side down, on a work surface, then run a skewer through them). Place on the grill and cook, turning occasionally, until the potatoes are lightly browned and tender, about 15 minutes. Transfer to a platter.

In a large bowl, whisk together the mustard, vinegar, the remaining ½ cup olive oil, the remaining scallions, and salt and pepper to taste. Slide the potatoes off the skewers into the mustard mixture and toss to coat. Serve immediately.

Skewering blanched little potatoes and grilling them until tender gives them a nice smoky undertone. Get a good red wine vinegar for the dressing, which is made creamy with lots of Dijon mustard.

SOURCES

ARMANDINO'S SALUMI

309 Third Avenue South
Seattle, WA 98104
206-621-8772
www.salumicuredmeats.com
Cured meats made by my dad

ARTHUR AVENUE CATERERS

2344 Arthur Avenue
Bronx, NY 10458
866-2-SALAMI (272-5264)
718-295-5033
www.arthuravenue.com
Cured meats, specialty items, and cheeses

BIANCARDI MEATS

2350 Arthur Avenue
Bronx, NY 10458
718-733-4058
Fresh meat, game, and house-cured meats

CITARELLA

2135 Broadway
New York, NY 10023
212-874-0383
www.citarella.com
Fish and shellfish of all types

D'ARTAGNAN

280 Wilson Avenue
Newark, NJ 07105
800-327-8246
www.dartagnan.com
Fresh meat, game, and poultry

DEAN & DELUCA

560 Broadway
New York, NY 10021
800-2221-7714; 212-226-6800
www.deandeluca.com
Cured meats, cheese, olive oil, vinegar, and specialty produce

DIPALO

200 Grand Street
New York, NY 10013
212-226-1033
Italian cheese (including eighty-five types of pecorino), cured meats, olives, olive oil, vinegar, and pasta

FAICCO'S

260 Bleecker Street
New York, NY 10014
212-243-1974
Cured meats, pasta, oil, and vinegar

FORMAGGIO KITCHEN

244 Huron Avenue
Cambridge, MA 02138
888-212-3224; 617-354-4750
www.formaggiokitchen.com
*Cheese, olive oil, vinegar, pasta, and other
specialty foods*

GRATEFUL PALATE

888-472-5283
www.gratefulpalate.com
*Olive oil, vinegar, wine, and Bacon of the
Month Club*

HERITAGE FOODS USA

P.O. Box 827
New York, NY 10150
212-980-6603
www.heritagefoodsusa.com
*Heritage turkeys and other meats (Heritage is the
sales and marketing arm of Slow Foods USA)*

JAMISON FARM

171 Jamison Lane
Latrobe, PA 15650
800-237-5262
www.jamisonfarm.com
High-quality lamb

KALUSTYAN'S

123 Lexington Avenue
New York, NY 10016
800-352-3451; 212-685-3451
www.kalustyans.com
*Mediterranean and Middle Eastern ingredi-
ents, as well as an amazing range of international foods and products, including fresh kaffir
lime leaves*

MANICARETTI

Mail order available through Market Hall
Foods; see below
www.manicaretti.com
*Imports many of the specialty products used
in our restaurants, including bottarga, estate-
produced olive oils and vinegars, high-quality
grains and rices, and superb pasta*

MARKET HALL FOODS

5655 College Avenue
Oakland, CA 94618
888-952-4005
www.markethallfoods.com
*Olive oil, vinegar, fennel pollen, fregola and
other pastas, and a wide variety of other
Italian and international foods and products*

MURRAY'S CHEESE SHOP
257 Bleecker Street
New York, NY 10014
888-692-4339; 212-243-3289
www.murrayscheese.com
Extensive cheese selection, as well as olives, oil, pasta, vinegar, and other imported specialty items

NIMAN RANCH
866-808-0340
www.nimanranch.com
Free-range and organic meats

PENZEYS SPICES
19300 West Janacek Court
P.O. Box 924
Brookfield, WI 53008
800-741-7787
www.penzeys.com
High-quality spices of all kinds, including brown mustard seeds

TODARO BROS.
555 Second Avenue
New York, NY 10016
877-472-2767
www.todarobros.com
Wide variety of Italian and other international products

VINO E OLIO
877-846-6365
www.vino-e-olio.com
Beans, cheese, coffee, mushrooms, pasta, truffles, oil, vinegar, and other specialty items

ZINGERMAN'S
422 Detroit Street
Ann Arbor, MI 48104
www.zingermans.com
Cheese, olive oil, vinegars, produce, and other specialty items

WWW.ITALIANKITCHEN.COM
For my absolute favorite stuff, please check out my own personal equipment (including a piastra) and kitchen tool line here

INDEX